ONE-HIT WONDERS

Fantastic and Lesser-Known Heroes from the Bible Who Will Enhance Your Relationship With God

SUSIE SHELLENBERGER
& BILLY HUDDLESTON

dustjacket

Published by Dust Jacket Press
One-Hit Wonders: Fantastic and Lesser-Known Heroes from the Bible Who Will Enhance Your Relationship With God / Susie Shellenberger and Billy Huddleston

ISBN: 978-1-953285-87-4

Dust Jacket Press
P.O. Box 721243
Oklahoma City, OK 73172
www.dustjacket.com

Cover & interior design: D.E. West - emoondesigns.com w/ Dust Jacket Creative Services

Printed in the United States of America

DEDICATION

To Steve and Vickie Stearman,
my cousins who faithfully and consistently
pray for and support my calling into ministry.
I love you.
—Susie

To Yvonne Chalfant,
whose life and love for the Word has taught
me more than she'll ever know.
—Billy

CONTENTS

INTRODUCTION

One-hit wonders.

The music world is full of them. In fact, some of the most popular songs originated from artists who only became household names because of that one-hit single.

Although their popularity soared overnight, the peak of their fame amounted to just a single three-minute song. Popular—then never again.

There are also literary one-hit wonders, along with inventions that are one-hit wonders.

We find several spiritual one-hit wonders in the pages of Scripture. When we engage in actions that are directed and empowered by God, they might seem like one-hit wonders to the world, but if God is in charge, their influence will endure eternally.

Let's spend time with some incredible one-hit wonders from the Bible.

ONE-HIT WONDER: HENN TAN

In 1984, Singaporean one-hit wonder Henn Tan was appointed as the director of operations for Sanshin Electronics, an agent for NEC Semiconductors, where he oversaw the company's operations in Southeast Asia. Tan left the company in 1995 and acquired a small family-owned business that traded in electronic parts called Trek.

Tan changed the whole structure of the business to focus on providing technology-driven engineering solutions to businesses.

In 2000, Tan and his team explored different ways to create a data storage device using the USB interface. This led to the invention of the USB flash drive. Tan lives off the success of his invention and has not invented anything else since. He was a one-hit wonder.

CHAPTER ONE

(2 Kings 13:20-21)

Good Bones

What will people remember you for after you die? Take a seat and enjoy Elisha's remarkable legacy that endures long after his time on earth has passed.

We've all attended funerals. While it's heart-breaking to say farewell to a loved one, the funeral can also serve as a celebration of the deceased's life—particularly if that life was well-lived.

We're meeting a man today who interrupted his own funeral. Actually, he never had a funeral; he interrupted his burial.

Let's take a look:

**"So, Elisha died, and they buried him.
Now Moabite raiders would enter
the land in the spring. [21] As they were
burying a man, they saw raiders. So
they threw the man into the tomb of**

Elisha. When the man touched the bones of Elisha, he came to life and stood on his feet." (2 Kings 13:20-21 MEV)

What?!?

Elisha died.

You might know that Elisha was a powerful prophet in the Old Testament. He was a protégé of another notable prophet: Elijah. Their ministries—and even their names—were similar.

Elisha enjoyed a fulfilling ministry and life. By reading about him in Scripture, it's clear he lived,

moved

and worked

in God's supernatural power.

Just before we learn of his death—in the same chapter of 2 Kings 13—we see God, through Elisha, granting victory to the Israelites over King Aram three times. (See 2 Kings 13:18-19.)

Next, we come to verse 20:

"So, Elisha died, and they buried him. (2 Kings 13:20 NLT).

He was performing miracles through God's power right up to his death.

Second Kings 13:16 tells us that Elisha became ill and died from the sickness he had.

Even in his sickness—during his last days—he was still being used by God.

What a way to go!

Wouldn't it be wonderful if our story was remembered for having the same steadfast faith: We served God until the end—using every moment, even in our final days, to be used by Him?

Right now would be a great time to stop reading.

What? I just began this chapter!

I understand. But put the book aside for a few minutes. Grab a cup of coffee or a soft drink and have a conversation with Jesus. Ask Him if there's anything in your life that's stopping Him from using you right now. If you ask Him, He WILL answer! If God brings something to your mind, go ahead and give that area to Him. Tell Him you genuinely want Him to use you to glorify His name.

Ready to keep moving? Let's go!

**"So Elisha died, and they buried him.
Now Moabite raiders would enter the land
in the spring. 21 As they were burying a
man, they saw raiders.
So they threw the man into the tomb of
Elisha. When the man touched
the bones of Elisha, he came to
life and stood on his feet."
(2 Kings 13:20-21 MEV)**

Moabite raiders invaded the land every spring. Just as flowers bloomed, plants sprouted from the ground, and fruit buds appeared on the trees—just when God's people saw crops growing and their hard work paying off—the Moabites would rush in and take everything.

God often uses non-believing people to wake up the believers.

We see this pattern throughout the Old Testament. God's chosen people, the Israelites, serve Him and are blessed, but they become complacent, start to coast, lower their guard, and begin worshiping idols.

It's when we receive blessings from God that we need to stay alert. Usually, when blessed, we become complacent. What happens when we let our guard down? The enemy invades God's territory—an area of your life once dedicated to the Lord.

It's a vicious cycle-that happens over

and over

and over

again

and

again

and . . . okay, you get the picture.

Those Pesky Enemies

Here in 2 Kings, God uses the Moabites to get the attention of His people. At other times, He used the Hivites, Jebusites, Parasites, the Pepsi-Lites, and Mosquito Bites.

The bottom line is that God *will* get your attention. Let's avoid letting non-believers be the ones who prompt us to listen to Him. Instead, let's develop a lifestyle of listening to our Father.

Question: How well do you recognize the voice of God? When He speaks to you, are you able to hear Him? You might be thinking, *He never speaks.* Oh, but He does!

We can verify it through His voice in the Bible! He has spoken, and He will continue to speak.

Could it be that you don't recognize His voice?

How do I learn His voice?

By spending time with Him.

Reading the Bible.

Praying.

Let's return to the Moabites. God is using this violent group of people to grab the attention of His children because they have pushed Him aside.

We see the same thing happening to Gideon in Judges 6:1-14. The Midianites raided their land every

single
spring.

The Midianites were so brutal that the Israelites hid in caves, went deep into the mountains, and took cover wherever they could.

Here's the description from Scripture about how mean the Midianites were:

"The Israelites did evil in the Lord's sight. So the Lord handed them over to the Midianites for seven years. The Midianites were so cruel that the Israelites made hiding places for themselves in the mountains, caves, and strongholds. Whenever the Israelites planted their crops, marauders from Midian, Amalek, and the people of the east would attack Israel, camping in the land and destroying crops as far away as Gaza. They left the Israelites with nothing to eat, taking all the sheep, goats, cattle, and donkeys. These enemy hordes, coming with their livestock and tents, were as thick as locusts; they arrived on droves of camels too numerous to count. And they stayed until the land was stripped bare. So Israel was reduced to starvation by the Midianites. Then the Israelites cried out to the Lord for help."
(Judges 6:1-6 NLT)

Pitiful, isn't it?

Everything they had worked so hard to plant, sow, and grow was stolen by the cruel Midianites. To say the Midianite raiders were a terrifying group is a gross understatement. When God appeared to Gideon, Scripture tells us that the Lord's angel found him in a wine press. What was he doing there? Scripture says he was threshing wheat.

But the problem is . . . you can't thresh wheat in a wine press. In biblical times, a wine press was like a large, round bucket. You'd stand inside that bucket and stomp on the grapes.

A large open space was essential for threshing wheat. You needed to toss the wheat into the air, allowing the wind to blow away the chaff while the wheat fell to the ground. Gideon was so terrified that he was trying the impossible—threshing the small amount of wheat he had—in a wine press.

LOTS OF QUESTIONS

Let's go back to our Scripture for today:

"So Elisha died, and they buried him. Now Moabite raiders would enter the land in the spring. As they were burying a man, they saw raiders. So they threw the man into the tomb of Elisha. When the man touched the bones of Elisha, he came to life and stood on his feet." (2 Kings 13:21 MEV)

Who were they? They weren't the raiders. They *saw* the raiders. These buriers were Israelites. But who were they?

Were they family members of the deceased?

Were they friends?

Could they have been the dead man's neighbors?

We don't know.

We have absolutely no details about these buriers.

And who was the dead man? Was he a community leader? Was he someone's father? A brother? Just a guy off the street? We don't know.

What we *do* know is that "a man" died and "they" were burying him.

MORE INFO PLEASE

Not a lot to go on here.

A man died.

Men buried him.

We aren't even sure how far along they were in the burial process. Had he been covered with the usual balms and spices used for burials? Had they finished digging the grave? We know they didn't complete the *burial* because Scripture says, "as they were burying..." Unfortunately, they didn't have a local funeral home to help with this. They were on their own.

Perhaps they had just started digging into the side of a mountain. Maybe they had just broken ground. But as they worked, they saw raiding Moabites approaching quickly in the distance. The buriers were overcome with fear; they were panic-stricken.

If presented in a comic-book style, we'd see words like "Gasp!" "Yikes!" and "Gulp!" in the dialogue bubbles.

They knew the Moabites were coming for one reason

only: to raid. And they'd stop at nothing to get what they wanted. These buriers understood they'd never see another sunset if the raiders found them. So *these men* responded in fear!

"So they threw the man into the tomb of Elisha." (2 Kings 13:21 MEV)

Though survival was their top priority, they realized they couldn't leave the dead man on the ground. Still, they understood they lacked the time to bury him and make it out alive. So, they threw the dead man into a nearby tomb—which happened to be the burial place of the prophet Elisha.

And then a miracle happened! Let's read the rest of the Scripture:

"When the man touched the bones of Elisha, he came to life and stood on his feet." (2 Kings 13:20-21 MEV)

What?!?

And that's the end of the story. We definitely have a few unanswered questions: Did the guy make it out? If he did escape, how? Was he able to climb out? Did he just sit there in shock for a few hours? Was he terrified when he woke up next to a skeleton? Did he scream for help? How long was he in there?

Maybe we should simply focus on what we DO know. So, let's chat about Elijah and Elisha. To do that, we'll look at 2 Kings 2:1.

"The time had come for the Lord to take Elijah up to heaven in a whirlwind." (2 Kings 2:1 HCSB)

The prophet Elijah had an extraordinary ministry. Powered by God, he called fire down from heaven, burned a bull without matches or kerosene, and defeated 450 evil prophets of Baal. He multiplied flour and oil for a widow, and when her son died, he brought him back to life.

The miracles go on and on. But in 2 Kings 2:1, we see that he had reached the end of his time on earth. He didn't die—God took him to heaven in a whirlwind. Elijah was one of only two people in the Bible who didn't die. Enoch is the other. He was truly in love with his heavenly Father. They walked so closely together that God allowed him to simply walk right into heaven. What a way to go!

In 2 Kings 8-9, we see that Elijah and Elisha need to cross the Jordan before they are taken to heaven.

"Elijah took his cloak, rolled it up and struck the water with it. The water divided to the right and to the left, and the two of them crossed over on dry ground.
"When they had crossed, Elijah said to Elisha, 'Tell me, what can I do for you before I am taken from you?'
" 'Let me inherit a double portion of your spirit,' Elisha replied."
(2 Kings 2:8-9 NIV)

In other words, "Elijah, I can clearly see God manifested in every aspect of your life! And oh, Elijah, I desire that. I long for that. I want what I observe in your life. And I want double."

PEOPLE ARE WATCHING

It makes me wonder, *Am I living in a way that makes others want what they see?*

A few years ago, Billy and I shared speaking engagement at a family camp in East Tennessee. The event creators rotated our speaking schedules throughout the week, and God blessed us with wonderful services.

When I headed home and landed at the OKC airport, I took my luggage outside to the area where the airport shuttle vans were located. One of the drivers saw me coming and called my name in his thick Middle Eastern accent: "Shellenberger!"

I was stunned.

It had probably been almost a year since I'd ridden in his van.

"You have an amazing memory," I said.

He laughed and said, "You're the religious lady."

I smiled. "And you're my Muslim friend from Pakistan, right?"

"Yes, but I believe a few other things, too."

He wasn't pointing a finger at me or being mean: "Oh no—there's that religious lady."

His tone was sweet. His words were gentle and affirming.

He remembered our conversation about Jesus the last time I rode with him.

I climbed into his van, and we chatted on the way to my house. When we neared my home, I asked, "Is there anything I can pray for you about?"

"Yes," he said. "Three weeks ago, my father died. I wasn't able to be in Pakistan when he passed away. I miss him so much."

"I'm so sorry," I said. "I know the pain of losing a dad. Mine has been gone for three years, and I'll never stop missing him. I'm so glad Jesus understands our pain."

People are watching us.

Someone is watching your life.

It could be the grocery store cashier who rings up your purchases every week, a family member, or someone you work with. But someone is watching your actions, listening to your words, and evaluating your lifestyle.

Do they want what they see?

What a compliment for Elisha to say to Elijah, "I

want what I see. And I want a double portion of what you're living."

" 'You have asked a difficult thing,' Elijah said, 'yet if you see me when I am taken from you, it will be yours—otherwise, it will not.' "
(2 Kings 2:10 NIV)

In other words, it's not Elijah's decision, and he understands that. He can't give God's anointing to anyone; only God has that authority. That's precisely why the Israelites often messed up: They tried to do God's work in their own strength. "Hey, we want to choose our own kings. We don't need God to decide that for us. We can select and anoint whoever we want to be our leaders and priests."

God, however, specifically told the Israelites at the beginning of their journey to the Promised Land that only people from the tribe of Levi could serve as priests. If you weren't from the tribe of Levi, you couldn't be a priest.

In other words . . . wait for it . . .

if you didn't have Levi jeans, I mean genes . . .

bwahahaha

I couldn't help it.

I'm cracking myself up as I'm writing this.

Back to the important stuff.

Elijah spoke the truth to his protégé. "What you're asking isn't my decision. I truly don't have *any* authority.

Everything I've experienced and accomplished has been through the Lord's power. It's in His hands. He determines whom He will choose to anoint."

Let's keep reading:

"As they were walking along and talking together, suddenly a chariot of fire and horses of fire appeared and separated the two of them, and Elijah went up to heaven in a whirlwind.

"Elisha saw this and cried out, 'My father! My father! The chariots and horsemen of Israel!' And Elisha saw him no more. Then he took hold of his garment and tore it in two.

"Elisha then picked up Elijah's cloak that had fallen from him and went back and stood on the bank of the Jordan. He took the cloak that had fallen from Elijah and struck the water with it.

" 'Where now is the Lord, the God of Elijah?' he asked. When he struck the water, it divided to the right and to the left, and he crossed over.

"The company of the prophets from Jericho, who were watching said, 'The spirit of Elijah is resting on Elisha.' And they went to meet him and bowed to the ground before him."

(2 Kings 2:11-15 NIV)

Let's do some multiplication: This is affirmation x 2.

God confirms His anointing of Elisha. He split the river and crossed on dry ground, and the other prophets affirm that they witnessed it.

But is it double?

WE WANT TO KNOW

As we continue through 2 Kings, we definitely see God moving through Elisha in numerous miracles. But let's get back to the Scripture we began with:

"So Elisha died, and they buried him. Now Moabite raiders would enter the land in the spring. [21] As they were burying a man, they saw raiders. So they threw the man into the tomb of Elisha. When the man touched the bones of Elisha, he came to life and stood on his feet."
(2 Kings 13:20-21 MEV)

When Elijah asked Elisha what he wanted, Elisha replied that he wanted a double portion of God's presence and action within him. But now he's dead.

Did God answer that request? We know God anointed him, used him, and performed miracles through him, but twice as much as Elijah?

How do we quantify this? Shouldn't there be a way? Well, Bible scholars have said that we can count 14 main miracle events of Elijah in the Bible. *Fourteen*. That's a lot.

I'm not very good at math; I have never been. But I can add, subtract, multiply, and divide. It's those pesky word problems that leave me scratching my head.

I do know that 14 + 14 = 28.

Or if we choose to multiply: 14 x 2 = 28.

We can count 27 main event miracles of Elisha in the Bible.

If he had received the double portion of anointing that Elijah received, we would have seen 28 miracles.

Here's the issue: In 2 Kings 13, when we read that Elisha died and was buried, there are only 27 recorded miracles. We only have 27 instances where God acted through Elisha to perform a miracle.

Well, 27 is pretty good!

But that's NOT double.

And God isn't just pretty good.

Twenty-seven is not a double portion. No matter how we twist it or what kind of new math we use, it's still not a double portion. The promise was not granted.

Elisha died without receiving what he wanted—the double portion. There were twenty-seven miracles when Elisha died. God's Word is truth. Every promise He makes will be fulfilled.

There are promises based on His Word that He has placed within each one of us. And based upon His Word, we believe He is going to fulfill the promises He has given us. But there are times when we claim a certain promise, and then we wait, pray, wait more, pray more and. . . .

Well, sometimes we can't help wondering if the promise we're waiting on will never be fulfilled. Even as we pray harder and longer and hold on to our faith, it can still seem as though fulfillment is nowhere on the horizon.

If you're there now—be reminded that it's not over.

It's.

not.

over.

Come back to the story. Elijah's 14 miracles, which God performed through him, are recorded in Scripture. Elisha was promised a double portion, but at the time of his death, Elisha only received 27 miracles from God. He did not receive what had been promised.

HOLD ON

Even though Elisha died, God's promise did not. God doesn't forget, nor does He lie. God is always faithful, will always keep His word, and *will* have the final say.

Elisha died. Years passed. We see him buried in his final resting place—where he will decay, where his body will return to dust. The promise seems to be buried with him. And there his bones remain with 27 miracles until . . .

SOME guys—whoever they are—threw a man—whoever he was—into Elisha's tomb, where his body touched Elisha's bones and he came back to life!

What's the big deal?

Why does that matter?

Because that's 28.

Elisha died but God's promise didn't.

Hollywood can't create this, but God can.

Elisha's life had ended but God's promises hadn't.

God's promises are true.

His Word will never fail.

Stay encouraged. God means what He says, even when years go by and it seems like He's not doing anything. Don't give up. Don't you dare quit. Keep believing. You might not see it happening in this life, but through the eyes of faith, you can trust it.

You may feel as though God has forgotten. He hasn't. Maybe you're wondering if God's dreams for you will ever come to pass.

God always keeps His Word.

You've prayed so long and so hard for something you thought God would assure you would happen, and you're beginning to wonder. God is always trustworthy.

What He says He will do—He does.

What He says will happen—happens.

Maybe you just need to be reminded.

God is *not* finished.

What a strange story. Two weird, obscure, yet relevant verses with a timeless truth.

GOING DEEPER:

- Are you living your life in such a way that people want what they see?
- Identify a time when God answered a specific prayer for you.
- Are you discouraged about something specific in your life that you feel God hasn't answered?

God keeps His promises.

It's when we're being blessed by God that we need to keep our guard up.

Someone is observing your actions, hearing your words, and assessing your lifestyle.

ONE-HIT WONDER: MARGARET MITCHELL

Margaret wrote just one novel during her lifetime, published in 1936. *Gone With the Wind* earned her the National Book Award for Fiction as well as the Pulitzer Prize for Fiction. She was an American journalist who published several articles but is primarily known for her one Civil War book. She was a literary one-hit wonder.

CHAPTER TWO

(Acts 16:6-40)

What's Up with Purple?

We all have our favorite color. Oftentimes, we decorate a room with that swatch or even have a few pieces of clothing in that color. But purple was much more than a color to Lydia—it was her livelihood.

What we do for God, lasts eternally. When we do something that's God-directed and God-empowered, it may appear to be a one-hit wonder to the world, but if God's in charge, the influence will last eternally.

Lydia was just such a person.

She was a one-hit wonder, but her story is still being talked about today, centuries later.

Let's set the scene: The apostle Paul, Silas, Luke and Timothy were on a missionary journey. We'll pick up part of their journey in Acts 16:6-12:

"Next they traveled through Phrygia and Galatia because the Holy Spirit had told them not to go into the Turkish province of Asia Minor at that time. Then going along the borders of Mysia they headed north for the province of Bithynia, but again the Spirit of Jesus said no. So instead they went on through Mysia province to the city of Troas.

"That night Paul had a vision. In his dream he saw a man over in Macedonia, Greece, pleading with him, 'Come over here and help us.' Well, that settled it. We would go to Macedonia, for we could only conclude that God was sending us to preach the Good News there.

"We went aboard a boat at Troas, and sailed straight across to Samothrace, and the next day on to Neapolis, and finally reached Philippi, a Roman colony just inside the Macedonian border, and stayed there several days."

(Acts 16:6-12 TLB)

Paul and his team received a powerful call to mission work and responded obediently to God's leading. But imagine their surprise when they arrived in the major city of Philippi and found there was no synagogue.

You see, Jewish law required ten males to establish a synagogue. There weren't ten God-fearing Jews in the entire city. In Paul's vision, there was a man calling him to Macedonia. If I were him, I'd be wondering, *Where's THAT man? Your prayers have been answered! I'm answering the call.*

To make things even more complicated, inscribed on the arches outside Philippi was a ban on bringing unrecognized religions into the city. This might explain why there was a Jewish prayer meeting happening outside the city, on the riverbank.

Having been trained by the Jews to be a leader *among* Jews, Paul was well acquainted with their views of women. The rabbis were known to say, "It's better that the words of the Law be burned than be delivered to a woman."

Paul's willingness to speak with these women shows he didn't hold that view. However, the absence of a synagogue, no influence in the city, a ban on religion, and a prayer meeting by a riverbank didn't seem to be the ingredients for a powerful revival.

So often we see things only from our perspective.

There was an organization in Montana that aimed to reduce the wolf population by offering $5,000 for each wolf caught alive. Two old-timers, Sam and Jed, decided they could make good money trapping wolves. They searched the mountains, followed tracks, and set traps. This went on for several days but yielded no results.

One night, Sam woke up to find they were surrounded by wolves. Their eyes glowed red in the flickering light of the campfire, their white teeth bared and shining in the moonlight, and their back legs poised to pounce. Sam nudged Jed and said, "Wake up, Jed! We're gonna be rich!"

What you and I might see as dangerous or hostile could be an opportunity for the kingdom of God. In the words of Mordechi to Esther from the Old Testament:

"And who knows but that you have come to your royal position for such a time as this?" (Esther 4:14 NIV)

If Paul had looked for a new plan or gimmick, he would've bailed on Phillipi. But Paul understood that serving God is always about our faithfulness, not the results.

You might be in a place like Paul. You look at the things around you and ask, "Am I in the right place, God? Am I doing what you want me to?"

The circumstances may be overwhelming. Don't be too quick to throw in the towel. As we are about to find out, just one convert can make all the difference.

This specific call at this specific time in Paul's life (known as the "Macedonian Call") was *not* about huge numbers. There was only one convert at first—a woman named Lydia. She was a one-hit wonder.

But the Lord used her greatly to help Paul. We don't know much about Lydia. We know she was from Thyatira, a city known for shiny bronze and brass, and purple cloth. Lydia was a businesswoman who made and sold the expensive purple fabric.

Purple's not a color you can ignore.

These days, we're used to being able to get any color we want. You can take your purple cushion cover to Home Depot, they'll scan it into a machine and match paint exactly the same color. If you want a shirt or a blouse in a shop, they usually have all the colors and sizes available. If not, they'll order it for you.

It didn't used to be like that. Dyes were natural, not synthetic, and the purple dye was made from a juice found in tiny amounts in shellfish. It took thousands of crustaceans to produce a yard or two of purple cloth. So it was very expensive. It was a statement of status and wealth—like the Louis Vuitton purse or the Rolex watch of Roman times.

And that's what Lydia was selling: The color purple—purple cloth and purple robes—she was selling the power of purple. She wasn't local; she was from Thyatira, a town well known for making purple cloth. She seemed to be the head of her household; there wasn't a husband around. She was a traveling trader. And if she was a seller of purple, she wasn't poor because she couldn't have afforded her stock.

She wasn't Jewish, but she believed in God—and she worshipped God. Since she was a Gentile, her exposure to a traditional synagogue would have been very limited, but here at the riverbank, she found a place where she belonged. As Paul spoke—the Bible says that she listened and opened her heart. The Greek word here for *listen* indicates a continuing process.

In other words, Lydia had been listening to those at the riverbank and growing in her devotion to God, but that day Paul led her a little further down the road of understanding who God was and how He had sent Jesus. Paul was in the right place, at Phillipi on a riverbank with a group of women, and Lydia was in the right place listening to Paul.

But in that moment, she believed the word she had heard.

That's what it means when Scripture says, "she opened her heart to pay attention."

She was taking the next step in her spiritual journey, and that step was trusting Christ as her Savior. How exciting that Lydia was the first European convert to Christianity!

The missionaries ended up at her house again. I really think the ministry they received in verse 15 by staying at Lydia's house was a surprise blessing. Let's take a look:

"She was baptized along with all her household and asked us to be her guests.

" 'If you agree that I am faithful to the Lord,' she said, 'come and stay at my home.'

"And she urged us until we did."
(Acts 16:15 TLB)

Given her business and the high price purple cloth could command, her home was likely one of the nicer ones in Thyatira. She *willingly* shared what she had and demonstrated the spiritual gift of hospitality.

For Paul, Silas, and Luke to refuse her offer of hospitality would mean that they did NOT believe she had accepted Christ as her Savior.

Again, Lydia didn't just open her heart; she opened her home. Let's look at verse 40:

> **"Paul and Silas then returned to the home of Lydia, where they met with the believers and preached to them once more before leaving town. (Acts 16:40 TLB)**

The ministry in this verse was an essential necessity. After Paul and the crowd left Lydia, they cast out a demon and were arrested for doing so. God sent an earthquake that released them from prison, they were used by the Lord to convert a jailer and his family, and they reappeared before the government to exercise their rights as Roman citizens.

It was a busy couple of days for these men.

As they left Philippi, they might have discussed how difficult it had been, how they were hurt physically, emotionally, mentally, and possibly even spiritually.

Then Silas might have said, "You know what we need is a place to rest and recharge." Luke could have chimed in, "I know the perfect place. Remember how nice it was at Lydia's; how hospitable she was? Let's go there."

The word *hospitality* is a kind of hospital.

Now we rarely combine those two words in our culture because the mental images they create are so different. But a hospital is a place away from your home that's meant to bring healing and wholeness.

Hospitality is about using your home and your presence to bring emotional, mental, and spiritual healing to others. Maybe you've heard the saying that a man's home is his castle. Sadly, that's how many of us have started living—in fortresses of gated communities, with unlisted numbers, guarding our privacy, and isolating ourselves.

God did NOT design us like that.

We were made for community.

Here's the proof: Look at whom Paul and Silas encouraged—the brothers. Just ~~25~~ twenty-five verses ago, there were no men. Where'd the brothers come from? They had to come from Lydia and her evangelistic efforts.

Her home was a statement of her wealth and success. Then it became a mission outpost for some traveling missionaries. Now it's a church.

Home = wealth and success

Home = mission outpost

Home = church

Her home was a statement of her wealth and success. Then it became a mission outpost for some traveling missionaries. Ultimately, it became a church. The missionaries encouraged the brothers at the church, but how much were they encouraged because of the partnership that had taken place?

Lydia was using her gifts and possessions to start the church at Phillipi.

Paul was using his gifts and ability to exhort, encourage, and build the church spiritually.

They were in community—working together, each with their gifts and abilities.

That's a great picture of the church.

Lydia showed courage and steadfastness when she opened her house to these men of God. Remember, the prevailing spirit in Philippi was one of persecution and violence toward those preaching and teaching Christ. But her home became a *haven* for Paul and house fellowship began.

THE CHURCH BIRTHED IN EUROPE

The door to ministry in Europe opened. Despite her social status, she humbled herself and prepared to be recognized as a believer who ministered to the needs of God's anointed men.

Lydia was a one-hit wonder. But what an incredible difference a one-hit wonder can make when God does the empowering!

Through her hospitality, God opened the door for ministry in Europe!

Wow. Let's desire to have a heart like Lydia's; a heart longing for the things of God, to worship Him and to use everything He has given us for the benefit of His kingdom.

GOING DEEPER

- **Are you striving to BE the church?**
- **How would you describe your home? Is it a "secluded fortress" or a "sanctuary for hurting souls"? Please explain.**
- **Are you using your gifts and abilities to do what you can--right where you are?**
- **Are you listening to God in a way that helps you take the next steps in your spiritual journey?**

The circumstances may be overwhelming. Don't be too quick to throw in the towel.

But in that moment, she believed the word she had heard.

Hospitality is about using your home and your presence to bring emotional, mental, and spiritual healing to others.

ONE-HIT WONDER: BOBBY McFERRIN

DON'T WORRY BE HAPPY!

The music world is full of one-hit wonders. In fact, some of the most popular songs came from artists who only became a household name because of that one hit single.

Let's go back to 1988. Do you remember the fun song "Don't Worry, Be Happy"? Bobby McFerrin wrote the catchy little song, but he didn't do anything noteworthy afterward. It was definitely a one-hit wonder.

CHAPTER THREE

(John 6:1-14)

Weird Name, Weirder Story

He didn't have much, but he used what he had—and what a difference it made for an entire country.

We're starting this chapter with a dare. In fact, let's call it a double-dog dare! Take a few minutes and google "ShamWoW Commercial." Seriously. Get online and watch this. Now.

Did you watch it?

The man in the video is Vince Offer Shlomi. One day out of the blue,

Vince stepped into people's living rooms throughout the nation—and ShamWOW!

An opportunity arrived, and he stepped into it. Someone tapped him on the shoulder, and he said yes.

We never knew anything about him before then. And we don't know much about him SINCE then. He was a one-hit wonder. His commercial kind of reminds me of a man in the Bible named Shamgar.

If we made a video about this Bible hero, we could certainly title it "ShamWOW!" Like Vince, he too, saw an opportunity arise, and he stepped into it.

Let's set the stage:

Before Israel had kings, they had judges. And the Old Testament Book of Judges introduces us to these various judges. We know a lot about some of them—Samson for example.

You might be familiar with the story of Samson, who used a jawbone of a dead animal to kill 1,000 Philistines—and had one incredible feat after another. He was a larger-than-life hero in the Bible. His life was full of adventure and intrigue. He also had romantic escapades that brought him trouble many times and eventually led to his downfall.

We know quite a bit about a couple of other judges such as Deborah and Gideon. But we know very little about some of the other judges:

Tola, Jair,

Jephthah, Ibzan,

Elon, Abdon,

Othniel, Ehud, and Shamgar.

The Bible is filled with people who heard God's voice, stepped out in faith, followed His call, and made history. We read about one such judge in the Old Testament, in the Book of Judges, chapter 3, verse 31.

"The next judge after Ehud was Shamgar (son of Anath). He once killed six hundred Philistines with an ox goad, thereby saving Israel from disaster."
(Judges 3:31 TLB)

Now you might see the connection to the earlier reference I made, because after reading about Shamgar, my mind goes to ShamWOW! Shamgar was a minor judge and not a major figure in the chain of power for the people of Israel. (And by the way, the meaning of "judge" then meant one who would defend the people.)

Shamgar, son of Anath, came after the judge Ehud. Using a cattle prod, Shamgar killed 600 Philistines and saved the country of Israel!

ShamWOW!

That's incredible. Amazing.

Shocking. Tremendous.

Stunning. Marvelous. Fascinating.

Any positive adjective you can think of fits perfectly here. He was unquestionably a one-hit wonder empowered by God. We know nothing about him before or after the heroic feat he achieved.

He just chose to step out and trust the Lord, take Him at His word, and his name was forever recorded in the Bible.

HIS WEAPON

A cattle prod was his weapon of choice. That was all he had—a stick. But with God on his side, that was all he needed!

He slew 600 Philistines and saved Israel.

History records it as what a man did. But clearly it could only be recorded as what our almighty God did!

I can just imagine—600 men, whether they were trained soldiers or not—600 men is 600 men! And I don't think they were each politely waiting their turn to fight. They were *all* coming at him. And when the dust cleared—Shamgar was the last man standing—and the nation of Israel was saved!

This was miraculous.

He was called, chosen and used by God.

Let's look at Matthew 22:14 to see what Jesus said about those who are called:

"For many are called, but few are chosen."
(Matthew 22:14 KJV)

Many are called, but few listen—pay attention to—or respond to the call. For whatever reason, some choose not to follow God's prompting and His will in their lives. They might be good people. They might know the Scriptures. They could come from wealthy families. Their qualifications may be many. But God is *not* seeking someone's credentials; He's looking for obedience.

He doesn't always call the qualified. He qualifies those He calls.

God is looking for someone to step up to the plate and hit the ball!

Shamgar was that person. He recognized the need and took action. He didn't make excuses: "I don't have the right degree. I don't have experience in this specific area. I need to train first. No one has really asked me to complete this task. I'll pray for God to raise someone up to meet this need."

No. He recognized the need and simply rose to the occasion. Oh, what God can do with someone who is truly, totally, 100-percent available!

You see, there are some things we don't need to pray about. Several years ago, I (Susie) moved from Oklahoma City to Colorado Springs, Colo. Before I even made the move, I began praying, "Lord, show me quickly which church to join and how You want me to serve."

I didn't want to church-hop very long, nor did I want to wait to get involved. After visiting one particular church, I knew that was where God wanted me. I met with one of the pastors and he asked me to pray about starting a new Sunday school class. "We have a need," he said. "There's a hole we'd like ~~need~~ to fill. Please pray about starting a class and teaching it."

My response was, "I don't have to pray about it. When do you want me to start?" You see, I had already prayed about God leading me to a church in which I could serve. He was simply answering my prayer. Why would I need to keep praying about it? He had made it clear.

I believe there are some things we simply don't need to pray about. I think joining a church is one of those.

If you're regularly attending a Bible-preaching church and being spiritually fed there, it just makes sense to join.

Here's What's Needed

Shamgar saw the need. He didn't have to pray about it. The evil Philistines were coming his way. *Ohhhh, I hope God will raise someone up to do something.* "God, I'll pray and fast for three days, and You tell me what to do. . . ."

No, there's a need. I'm serving God, so I'll rise to the occasion and trust Him to equip me. Again, he could've made excuses: "I don't have any weapons. I need an army to battle 600 Philistines! I need to recruit soldiers and quickly get them trained. ***I*** need to get ***myself*** trained!"

It's hilarious that all Shamgar had was an oxgoad. An oxgoad was simply a stick. A stick! We'd think a simple stick would be about as useful as a ShamWOW when facing an army of enemies.

But when a simple piece of wood is empowered by Jehovah God, the possibilities are endless. Remember what God did when all Moses had was a rod? God empowered that piece of wood to become a living snake, didn't He! The most ordinary items—when placed in God's hands—become extraordinary!

Did David kill Goliath with a grenade? A gun? A sword? No. It was a simple, everyday slingshot. God took the ordinary and empowered it to be extraordinary. And He does the very same thing with people.

David was simply a shepherd boy with only a sling. And Shamgar was just one man armed only with an oxgoad—facing 600 enemies.

SAD BUT TRUE

Mark 10:17-22 tells the story of the man approaching Jesus with a question:

" 'Good Teacher, what must
I do to get eternal life?' "
"Jesus said, 'You know the
commandments: Don't murder, don't
commit adultery, don't steal, don't lie,
don't cheat, honor your
father and mother.' "
"He said, 'Teacher, I have—from
my youth—kept them all!'
"Jesus looked him hard in the eye—and
loved him! He said, 'There's one thing
left: Go sell whatever you own and give it
to the poor. All your wealth will then be
heavenly wealth. And come follow me.'
"The man's face clouded over. This was
the last thing he expected to hear, and
he walked off with a heavy heart. He was
holding on tight to a lot of things,
and not about to let go."
(Mark 10:27-22 The Message)

This man knew all about religion—but didn't know the One whom religion was all about.

Please notice this: Jesus looked him hard in the eye—and loved him!

Jesus was not going to tell him what he wanted to hear. He told him what He knew he *needed* to hear.

Jesus was asking for obedience—and in return, He was offering him everything: salvation, the peace that passes all understanding, love, joy, kindness, purpose, goodness, victory, faithfulness, and eternal life.

The man's face clouded over. This was the last thing he expected to hear, and he walked off with a heavy heart.

Saying YES to God is letting go. "Moses, throw down your rod."

"I need that, God. You're asking me to lead a million people through the wilderness, I need this walking stick."

Let it go, Moses.

"Slay the giant, David."

"All I have is this sling."

"Give it to Me, David. Watch what I'll do with it."

"Disciples, feed the crowd."

"Lord, there are thousands here. The only food we see is in the hands of a little boy—and it's not much."

"Bring him here. Give it to Me, son. Let it go. Watch what I'll do with your sack lunch."

Ohhh, there is power in letting go.

LET GO . . . AND LET GOD!

We often like to think that the people we read about in Scripture who have performed miracles have exceptional abilities. GOD is the One with the exceptional abilities. Everyone else has shortcomings. But guess what! God USES people who have shortcomings.

You see, when we allow God's purpose to be front and center, and we step out in faith and trust His ability over our own, there's nothing that can't be accomplished for His glory and His kingdom.

Shamgar was ready for the call of God when God called. Let's look at the Scripture again:

"The next judge after Ehud was Shamgar (son of Anath). He once killed six hundred Philistines with an ox goad, thereby saving Israel from disaster."
(Judges 3:31 TLB)

And that's it. Shamgar only gets two lines of Scripture, but it doesn't diminish the fact that this one-hit wonder was used in a mighty way by God and saved Israel. When God called him, he responded immediately. He didn't have to pray about it. He was prayed up! He was completely sold out to the things of God. And when the need arose, he didn't think twice.

God is still looking for men and women to be obedient and faithful.

What has God put in your heart to do for the Kingdom? Chances are, it's something bigger than you think that you were able to do on your own.

And that's the truth: On your own, it would never happen, and that's how you know it's from God.

God's dreams and plans for you are bigger than you can even imagine, and they all begin with one thing:

Yes, Lord.

Anything.

Any time.

Anywhere.

That's a commitment I made at 14 years of age, and I've never regretted it.

GOING DEEPER

- **Imagine yourself in Shamgar's sandals. If all you had was a stick, but you knew God was calling you to step up and protect His people, what would be running through your mind?**
- **Recall a time when you felt underqualified but still moved forward in faith to achieve something specific.**
- **Shamgar saved an entire country by stepping forward when God presented a need. Is there a specific area in your life, neighborhood, community, or church, where God has presented a need that, in faith, He could use you to fulfill?**

THE BIBLE IS FILLED WITH PEOPLE WHO HEARD GOD'S VOICE, STEPPED OUT IN FAITH, FOLLOWED HIS CALL, AND MADE HISTORY.

HE TOLD HIM WHAT HE KNEW HE NEEDED TO HEAR.

HE DOESN'T ALWAYS CALL THE QUALIFIED. HE QUALIFIES THOSE HE CALLS.

ONE-HIT WONDER: ANNA SEWELL

A lady named Anna Sewell wrote a book in 1877 about a horse you've probably heard of.

More than fifty million copies have been sold in fifty different languages.

But Anna Sewell passed away just five months after Black Beauty was published. Unfortunately, she was a one-hit wonder.

CHAPTER FOUR

(John 6:1-14)

Don't Forget About the Boy

Long before McDonald's came onto the scene, a boy and his fish sandwich made history.

"After this, Jesus crossed over to the far side of the Sea of Galilee, also known as the Sea of Tiberias. A huge crowd kept following him wherever he went, because they saw his miraculous signs as he healed the sick. Then Jesus climbed a hill and sat down with his disciples around him. (It was nearly time for the Jewish Passover celebration.)

"Jesus soon saw a huge crowd of people coming to look for him. Turning to Philip, he asked, 'Where can we buy bread to feed all these people?'

"He was testing Philip, for he already knew what he was going to do. Philip replied, 'Even if we worked for months,

we wouldn't have enough money to feed them!'
"Then Andrew, Simon Peter's brother, spoke up. 'There's a young boy here with five barley loaves and two fish. But what good is that with this huge crowd?'
" 'Tell everyone to sit down,' Jesus said. So they all sat down on the grassy slopes. (The men alone numbered about 5,000.)
"Then Jesus took the loaves, gave thanks to God, and distributed them to the people. Afterward, he did the same with the fish. And they all ate as much as they wanted. After everyone was full, Jesus told his disciples, 'Now gather the leftovers, so that nothing is wasted.'
"So they picked up the pieces and filled twelve baskets with scraps left by the people who had eaten from the five barley loaves."
(John 6:1-14 NLT)

Besides the resurrection, the feeding of the 5,000 is the only miracle recorded in all four Gospels. Each author tells the story a little differently, but the miracle itself remains the same. Still, there's a part of the story we might be tempted to overlook. Maybe it's because we're distracted by the miracle itself, which makes sense because it's incredible to see a small amount turn into much and a shortage become an abundance. Or maybe it's because it's so brief that it's easy to miss, and without this detail, the miracle wouldn't happen. It's a moment when Jesus and a young boy have an encounter that changes everything—not just for him, but for everyone there.

A LITTLE BACKGROUND

The days leading up to this had been busy. It was well into Jesus' second year of ministry, and His reputation was spreading quickly. No one had achieved what He had in such a short time—or ever, really. People everywhere wanted to be close to Him, to see or experience what only Jesus was doing. There was growing excitement around the carpenter from Nazareth and those closest to Him.

His disciples were also busy. Jesus sent them out in pairs to do everything He had been doing. As they traveled, they carried His authority, acted under that authority, and healed people of their troubles. Incredible things were happening, and news of it all spread throughout the region.

As the disciples returned to report everything that had happened to Jesus, they received heartbreaking news that John the Baptist had been beheaded. It was devastating. John had fulfilled his purpose by preparing the way, and now he had died a brutal death for standing up for what was right.

Jesus and the disciples were physically and emotionally exhausted. Their days had been busy, and now, with the upsetting news about John, Jesus invited them to take a well-deserved break with Him:

"Let's go off by ourselves to a quiet place and rest a while." (Mark 6:31 NLT)

This was a much-needed invitation to escape the crowd's demands and find solitude with Jesus. They eagerly accepted. It was exactly what they needed, and they gladly went with Him to the other side of the Galilee and up on a mountain to rest. However, the break was short-lived. Someone in the crowd must have overheard where they were headed. Having experienced a little bit of Jesus, they wanted more, and they would go the distance to get it.

Can we take a moment to reflect on the determination of this crowd? I've always been impressed by their willingness to do whatever it took to reach Jesus. Once you experience Jesus, the desire for more is natural. Psalm 34:8 says, **"Taste and see that the Lord is good. Oh, the joys of those who take refuge in Him!" (NLT).**

The psalmist invites us to personally experience God's goodness rather than just hear about it. We are encouraged to have a deep, personal encounter with Him, knowing that those who respond will find refuge and fulfillment in Him. That's what they had been doing. One by one, they experienced Jesus. They unloaded their cares and burdens onto Him, and He willingly relieved them of those things.

Now, having experienced relief—a different kind of rest—they did whatever they needed to do to get more, even if it meant walking around that lake to be where He was. I wonder, how determined are we to get more? What are we willing to do to receive it?

"When Jesus looked up and saw a great crowd coming toward him, he said to Philip, 'Where shall we buy bread for these people to eat?' He asked this only to test him, for he already had in mind what he was going to do."
(John 6:5-6 NIV)

As Jesus and the disciples sat on the hillside, Jesus looked up and saw a big crowd. It wasn't just a hundred people; it was 5,000 men. When you read "men," it's important to understand that it refers only to males, not women or children.

Sometimes in Scripture, "man" or "men" can mean mankind, including both males and females, young and old. The significance of this is that the actual crowd was probably much larger. Think about this: Whenever there are that many men, there are usually just as many women, if not more.

THAT'S A CROWD

With so many men and women present, there were probably many children as well. So, the total number of people was likely much higher. It probably doesn't matter, though. It's a huge crowd, and we get the sense that they quietly approached Jesus and the disciples. But you can't sneak up on Jesus; He saw them.

What exactly did Jesus see? A large crowd? Certainly, but He saw so much more. Mark 6:34 says that **"they were like sheep without a shepherd."**

The role of a shepherd is to watch over, feed, protect, lead, comfort, and keep the flock under his care. Sheep without a shepherd would be in great danger. They would scatter easily, wander into dangerous places, and ultimately become lost. Sheep cannot care for themselves. That's how Jesus perceives this crowd. He knew their determination to be where He was. In that, He perceived several things.

He understood their physical needs. The distance they had traveled was substantial to reach where He and the disciples were. During the journey, there would have been no drive-thru fast-food restaurants for a quick bite, nor any convenience stores to stop and buy a soda and a bag of chips as snacks. These men, women, and children had been following Jesus for some time, and He understood their physical needs. Although their physical needs were significant, Jesus recognized a greater need.

The *spiritual* needs of this crowd were more important than any meal. They didn't even realize what it was about Jesus that made them long for more. Yes, they were amazed by what they heard Him say and what they saw Him do—but there was more.

Something inside them yearned for what only Jesus could give. They might not have realized it, but their hearts were empty. Spiritually, they were starving to death, and Jesus was the only One who could satisfy that hunger. It's been said that every human heart has a God-shaped hole that only He can fill. This was the crowd's greatest need. And Jesus would supply what they needed.

Not only did Jesus understand their physical and spiritual needs, but He also took the opportunity to strengthen His disciples' faith and give them another chance to recognize who He truly was. Sadly, we are later told that they missed it.

"For they had not understood about the loaves, because their hearts were hardened." (Mark 6:52 NKJV)

AN OUTRAGEOUS QUESTION!

As the crowd drew closer, Jesus asked,

'. . . where shall we buy bread for these people to eat?" (John 6:5 NIV)

What an incredible question. This wasn't just a Sunday family lunch, nor was it a well-organized potluck for a church homecoming. Jesus and His disciples were alone on a hillside when thousands arrived unexpectedly. And Jesus wanted to feed them. With what? It was an overwhelming task, and yet Jesus was serious. He wasn't trying to make a joke. There was no sarcasm in His voice (or doubt, for that matter). He wanted to meet their physical need for food, so He set this task before the men. How would they respond? Philip spoke up.

With surprise in his voice, Philip answered Him, "Eight months' wages would not buy enough bread for each one to have a bite!" (John 6:7 NIV).

That's a substantial amount of money. It's large, and Philip knew it. That's why he chose that amount as his response. He was saying, "It's impossible, Jesus. You might as well just send them home!" As we follow the flow of the text, we see the crowd's determination, Jesus' compassion, and the disciples' doubt. Isn't it interesting that doubt was the first reaction of those who knew Jesus best—His followers? Yet they questioned the things He had asked them to do.

TIME OUT

Let's pause here for a moment. I want to admit that I'm guilty of the same thing. Honestly, I'm more guilty than the disciples were. There have been many times in my life when I felt like something was impossible, and the task before me was insurmountable. And on my own—it would be—but I know I'm not alone. He has proven to be faithful in every circumstance.

This is what I've found to be true:

"God is our refuge and strength, always ready to help in times of trouble." (Psalm 46:1 NLT)

Have you ever experienced this? There are many reasons to trust His ability. We see evidence of His faithfulness in our lives and in the lives of others. We've seen throughout history what He can do. Many of us have heard this story many times before, yet we still doubt. Let's not forget—though it's easy to judge—that these men were on a day-by-day journey with Jesus. Every day they spent with Him, every step they took, they were discovering who He was and what He was capable of. Philip's response was a natural one. Let's get back to the story.

After Philip's response, Andrew spoke up and said:

"There's a young boy here with five barley loaves and two fish. But what good is that with this huge crowd?" (John 6:9 NLT).

Once again, we can hear the doubt in his voice, but this time it was combined with action. Some of the disciples—at least Andrew—looked through the crowd to see what they had to work with. The search came up short: a young boy, five barley loaves, and two fish. The find didn't seem impressive or useful.

A young boy and what he had wasn't worth much. And it wasn't the best society had to offer. It was the food of the poor: bread made from barley, not wheat, and a few sardines. How far would that go among thousands? Again, this didn't seem like the solution to the impossible situation they were in.

JESUS, THE MIRACLE WORKER

However, what Andrew and Philip didn't realize was that Jesus works best in impossible situations. This problem wouldn't be solved by how much money they had in their ministry account or what type of bread they had in their baskets. Remember, we're told that Jesus

"asked this only to test him, for he already had in mind what He was going to do."
(John 6:6 NIV)

Before Andrew knew anything about a young boy with loaves and fish, Jesus knew he was there and had what was needed to accomplish something great. And Jesus chose to use him and his resources to do just that! The young boy made himself available, and because he was, Jesus chose to use him in an incredible way.

We all need to remember that we are chosen. In fact, this is nothing new to our time. Check out the apostle Peter's wise reminder:

"You are a chosen generation . . ."
(1 Peter 2:9 NKJV)

The world can be inhospitable, so it's no wonder Jesus prayed this prayer on our behalf:

"They do not belong to this world . . ."
(John 17:16 NLT)

Because of that, we might start to feel like we don't measure up to the standards of this world and feel out of place. So, be reminded that He has chosen you for a purpose. The question is, will you be available for that purpose? If you make yourself available, Jesus will use you to accomplish His will. And when He shows you what's required, you need to be willing to do whatever He asks. Yet even though His way is always best, He won't force it on you. Jesus gives you the freedom to choose—your way or His.

What would you have done? I've thought about it, and I would've felt pretty good about myself—out of all these people, my momma was the only one who sent me off with lunch. When Jesus asked for it, I would've been tempted to bargain. I could've worried that if I gave it all to Him, I wouldn't have any left and wouldn't get to eat. I'm pretty sure that's what I would've done. But this boy didn't.

THE GREATEST MIRACLE

The boy's response is the greatest miracle in this story. It's easy to get distracted by everything else, but don't overlook this. When Jesus asked him for his lunch—all five barley loaves and both small fish—he had no concern for himself. He didn't try to bargain or make a deal; he simply handed it over. It's almost as if you can hear his heart say, "If you have need of it, Jesus—take it all!"

The greatest miracle in any believer's life happens when they fully surrender to Jesus. It's human nature to hold onto things that give us comfort, security, or define our identity. We want to make our plans, keep our possessions, control our relationships, and chase our ambitions. This is the natural tendency of humankind; it's human nature. But too often, trying to stay in control leads to anxiety, fear, and false security. True peace only comes when we surrender to Him. Far from showing weakness, surrendering to Him is the ultimate act of strength and faith on our spiritual journey.

To surrender means yielding to His will instead of our own, trusting that His plans are greater than any we could create ourselves. When we're willing to be like that young boy and say, "If you need it, Jesus—take it all!" He will.

Check out this great instruction from the Old Testament that's so very relevant today:

"Trust in the Lord with all your heart and
lean not on your own understanding;
in all your ways submit to Him, and He will
make your paths straight."
(Proverbs 3:5-6 ESV)

True freedom is found when we surrender everything to Him without any strings attached. Have you done that? Are you living in that freedom?

AS MUCH AS YOU WANT

"Jesus took the loaves, gave thanks to God, and distributed them to the people. Afterwards, he did the same with the fish. And they all ate as much as they wanted." (John 6:11 NLT)

Because of this act of complete surrender, everyone there ate as much as they wanted. Not only that, in verse 12, it tells us they were filled, and in verse 13, there are twelve baskets filled with leftovers. All from five barley loaves and two small fish! If anyone left hungry that day, it was their own fault. Jesus had supplied the food—if they wanted to eat, they could have. If they wanted to be filled, they could have been. If it didn't happen, they had nobody but themselves to blame!

You can have as much of Jesus as you desire. That's truly one of the wonderful truths we learn from this story. It seems like we live in a time when nobody is willing to take responsibility. Whenever something goes wrong or things don't work out, it's always someone else's fault, their problem. This will never be the case in your relationship with Jesus. You are the only one who can take responsibility for and answer for it.

Everything necessary has been provided so we can become the people God intends us to be. Ultimately, it all depends on our willingness to surrender and live where He longs for us to be. I'll say it again—you can have as much or as little of Jesus as you want!

SO, DON'T FORGET ABOUT THE BOY

Whenever we read about the feeding of the five thousand, we often focus on Jesus, the crowd, or the disciples, and almost overlook the central character of the story. If it hadn't been for him, we wouldn't have this miracle. And we learn so much from his story.

It's probably safe to assume that no one in that crowd thought he mattered. They couldn't have known that what he was carrying in his basket, what his momma had sent with him, would become the provision for everyone that day. Certainly, they didn't realize that his story would be told for generations about the power of what Jesus can accomplish through an act of complete surrender. What an amazing story! Jesus performed the impossible through an overlooked kid in the middle of a huge crowd. The boy never received any glory from them; only Jesus did. But the story of his selfless act lives on as an example for everyone to follow.

Maybe today you feel small. Perhaps you feel like an insignificant part lost in the crowd. Or you might believe you have nothing to offer. The truth is, we never really know how or who the Lord will use in ways we could never imagine. All it takes is surrender. You know... it could be you. That's just the way He works.

> The greatest miracle in any believer's life happens when they fully surrender to Jesus.

GOING DEEPER

- **When you think about the feeding of the 5,000, what are some aspects of the story that stand out to you?**
- **What is your biggest challenge in fully surrendering to Jesus? Are there things you try to control or hold onto? How have you learned to deal with those things?**
- **Have you ever experienced a moment in your walk with Jesus when it felt like what you had was too small, but when you gave it to Jesus, you discovered it was more than enough?**
- **Write down what you need to surrender more fully to Him and journal a prayer that requests that surrender.**

If you make yourself available, Jesus will use you to accomplish His will.

Once you get a taste of Jesus, the desire for more is natural.

ONE-HIT WONDER: MACARENA

You may have danced to the hit song "Macarena" by the pop duo Los del Río, consisting of Antonio Romero and Rafael Ruiz. Although it was released in 1993, most people dance to the remix recorded in 1992.

Billboard ranked it number one on its list of "All-Time Latin Songs." However, despite Los del Rio's attempts to release another international hit, their "Macarena" masterpiece ultimately became a one-hit wonder.

CHAPTER FIVE

(Acts 12:12-15)

Knock, Knock

One teen girl + several prayer warriors +
a someone at the door =
the greatest knock-knock joke ever.

The only Rhoda I (Susie) am familiar with in real life is Rhoda Morgenstern. Do you remember her?

She was a TV sitcom star played by actress Valerie Harper. The show ran for five seasons, from 1974 to 1978.

It was a spin-off from "The Mary Tyler Moore" show.

I always thought it would be fun to meet Valerie, a great actress who passed away in 2019. But there's another Rhoda I'm looking forward to meeting when I get to heaven.

She's mentioned only once in Scripture, but what a wonderful woman of God she is! We find her at a prayer meeting in Acts 12:13-15. But before we actually meet her, let's set the scene.

"About that time King Herod moved against some of the believers and killed the apostle James (John's brother). When Herod saw how much this pleased the Jewish leaders, he arrested Peter during the Passover celebration and imprisoned him, placing him under the guard of sixteen soldiers." (Acts 12:1-4 TLB)

So, Herod was a people-pleaser—especially when it came to the crowds. He wasn't one to go against the culture around him. He wanted to be liked. He had a big ego, but his actions exposed his insecurities. Let's keep going.

"Herod's intention was to deliver Peter to the Jews for execution after the Passover. "But earnest prayer was going up to God from the church for his safety all the time he was in prison." (Acts 12:4-5 TLB)

Herod deviously planned to kill Peter. Herod was a manipulative, malevolent ruler who didn't want truth to obstruct his way of ruling however he desired.

"The night before Herod was to bring him out for his trial, Peter was sleeping between two soldiers.
"He was tied with two chains. Soldiers stood by the door and watched the prison." (Acts 12:6 NLV)

Notice how heavily he was guarded? Even while SLEEPING he was still chained between two soldiers—not guards—but soldiers (armed and trained). They weren't taking any chances with an escape attempt, were they? What happened next?

"All at once an angel of the Lord was seen standing beside him. A light shone in the building. The angel hit Peter on the side and said, 'Get up!'
"Then the chains fell off his hands. The angel said, 'Put on your belt and shoes!' He did.
"The angel said to Peter, 'Put on your coat and follow me.' "
(Acts 12: 7-8 NLV)

I love it! Peter was sleeping soundly in the midst of persecution. He probably knew that Herod planned to execute him, but Peter wasn't wringing his hands or pacing the jail floor (hard to do when you're chained to two soldiers anyway).

He's.

At.

Peace.

This reminds me of the stories of Daniel in the lion's den and Shadrach, Meshach, and Abednego.

Daniel: He had peace. He wasn't working on a strategy: "I'll move here, they'll go there, I'll dodge, I'll jump . . ."

Shadrack, Meshach, Abednego: "Is there a fire extinguisher in here?"

GENUINE PEACE

Where does this kind of peace come from?

1. Intimacy with God.

Make it your goal to know Him so well that you can find peace in the midst of persecution.

2. Trusting God.

This can be developed as a lifestyle. I've trusted Him in the past, and I can trust Him in the future. But of imminent importance, I can trust Him right now!

What would it take for you to live this way? What in your life would need to change? This is how we, as Christians, should strive to live.

Let's get back to Peter. It's funny that not only was he sleeping—but he was sleeping *soundly.* He was probably sawing logs. I imagine the soldiers rolling their eyes. "Seriously? This is not what I signed up for when I joined the army!"

Scripture shows us that Peter was sleeping so soundly that the angel couldn't wake him. The angel had already been speaking to him. Finally, the angel hit him. It took that kind of force to wake up Mr. Sleepy-Head! Then he yells, "Get up!"

Peter's mind was fuzzy. So the angel was extremely basic and very specific:

"The angel said, 'Put on your belt and shoes!' He did. The angel said to Peter, 'Put on your coat and follow me.' "Peter followed him out. He was not sure what was happening as the angel helped him. He thought it was a dream." (Acts 12:9 NLV)

Peter was still half asleep. "Am I dreaming? Am I sleepwalking? I don't understand."

"They passed one soldier, then another one. They came to the big iron door that leads to the city and it opened by itself and they went through. "As soon as they had gone up one street, the angel left him." (Acts 12:10 NLV)

Imagine the scene: This was the dead of night. Peter was walking through the darkened streets with the angel.

"Peter finally realized what had happened! 'It's really true!' he said to himself. 'The Lord has sent his angel and saved me from Herod and from what the Jews were hoping to do to me!' "
(Acts 12:11 TLB)

HOUSE PRAYER MEETING

While Peter was walking the streets, people had gathered to pray. These weren't half-hearted prayers; the believers were pouring out their hearts to God on Peter's behalf. So, Peter was out of jail, on the street—where did he go?

"After a little thought he went to the home of Mary, mother of John Mark, where many were gathered for a prayer meeting."
(Acts 12:11-12 TLB)

Mary of Jerusalem, a rich widow and mother of Mark the evangelist, owned a large and conspicuous house in the city, which she dedicated to the Lord. During the days of terrible persecution, the saints in Jerusalem regularly gathered in her lovely home not only to read and exegete the Word but also to pray for afflicted saints.

Now that Peter was out of prison, let's peek *behind the scenes* at what was happening while he was incarcerated.

"But earnest prayer was going up to God from the church for his safety all the time he was in prison." (Acts 12:5 TLB)

This prayer group at Mary's house had been diligently, passionately, fervently, and earnestly praying for Peter's release. Now, we see Rhoda enter the scene. Let's explore her role in this amazing story.

"He knocked at the door in the gate, and a girl named Rhoda came to open it." (Acts 12:13 TLB)

"And as Peter knocked at the door of the gate, a damsel came to hearken, named Rhoda." (Acts 12:13 KJV)

- The Living Bible calls Rhoda a girl.
- The Message says she was a young woman.
- The New Revised American Standard Bible says Rhoda was a maid.
- The New Century Version calls her a servant girl.
- The JB Phillips translation says she's a young maid.
- And the King James Version calls Rhoda a damsel.

A damsel was a female slave. We know she was young, but she was old enough to handle household duties—probably a teenage girl. In this not-for-TV sitcom, we learn that Rhoda remains the main character. Her lineage wasn't mentioned because she was a slave, and as a slave maid, she was considered unworthy of any genealogy.

KNOCK-KNOCK

Rhoda was fulfilling her humble duty of answering the door. She was handling the tasks that others found bothersome. She was used to this.

The name Rhoda means "rose, queen of flowers, pure and sweet." As a servant, she had no set hours. The fact that it was long past midnight when Peter arrived at Mary's house, and that Rhoda the slave answered the door, shows that she was willing to serve for long hours and late into the night.

The rest of this story can be described this way:

Knocked.

Mocked.

Shocked.

Peter Knocked:

**"He knocked at the door in the gate,
and a girl named Rhoda came to open it."
(Acts 12:13 TLB)**

Rhoda Shocked:

"Peter knocked at the outer entrance, and a servant named Rhoda came to answer the door. "When she recognized Peter's voice, she was so overjoyed she ran back without opening it and exclaimed, 'Peter is at the door!'" (Acts 12:13-14 NIV)

I love her excitement. Rhoda had been praying with this group of believers. Remember, they had been praying through the night. They started early that evening, and it wasn't quite dawn yet.

And Rhoda knew she was receiving a complete answer to her prayers. She couldn't hold back her joy. She was so happy, she was beside herself. Common sense would typically mean opening the door when someone knocks, but she understood she wasn't dealing with the ordinary anymore.

Rhoda was witnessing the supernatural: God had intervened and clearly performed a true miracle! That's the only explanation. She recognized Pete's voice and understood God's power.

Believers Mocked:

"They didn't believe her. 'You're out of your mind,' they said. "When she insisted they decided, 'It must be his angel. They must have killed him.' " (Acts 12:15 TLB)

It was easier to get out of prison than to get into this prayer meeting!

They didn't believe their prayers would be answered.

Rhoda's Prayer Meeting.

Knock, knock, knock.

"Please save Peter. Please set Peter free."

Knock, knock, knock.

"Oh, God, You know that Peter will be executed in the morning. Save him."

Knock, knock, knock.

Peter knocked and knocked and knocked. People were so busy asking God to deliver Peter that they didn't take a moment to recognize God's answer! No one answered the door, yet they all wondered who it was. Again, those present fervently prayed that God would deliver Peter. But they didn't really believe that God would do what they asked—or they would have jumped up exclaiming, "It must be God's answer!"

Do you ever find yourself praying this way?

You pour out your heart to God and convince yourself that you're trusting Him . . . but deep down—so far down in your soul that you're afraid to confront it—is the overwhelming doubt: *Is He really going to answer my prayer?*

How did the believers respond to Rhoda?

**" 'You're out of your mind,' they told her.
When she kept insisting that it was so,
they said, 'It must be his angel.' "
(Acts 12:14-15 NIV)**

"You're outta your mind!"

The King James Version says: "You're mad!"

Even though she was scorned, Rhoda kept insisting that they go to the door and see for themselves. She didn't back down; she showed boldness. This is amazing because she was a slave. Her young heart believed in God and the power of prayer. She didn't give up when she was ridiculed. It's one thing to be mocked by the world; it really hurts to be ridiculed by our Christian brothers and sisters!

Don't you want to grab the believers and say, "Are you kidding me right now? What have you been praying for? An angel? No. You've been praying for Peter's release!"

WHAT HAPPENED NEXT?

"But Peter kept on knocking, and when they opened the door and saw him, they were astonished.

"Peter motioned with his hand for them to be quiet and described how the Lord had brought him out of prison.

" 'Tell James and the other brothers and sisters about this,' he said, and then he left for another place."
(Acts 12:16-17 NIV)

Aren't you glad Peter was consistent? He kept knocking even when believers didn't respond. We'll face times when our Christian friends won't react the way we need them to. People will let us down and disappoint us. Don't give up. Keep knocking. God will always respond. It may not happen the way you expected, but

He

will

respond.

The believers were astonished. What? God really answers prayer?!?

Peter shared his story, emphasizing the significance of the believers hearing the specifics of how God answered their prayers.

Then Peter said, "Tell James and the other brothers and sisters about this."

In other words, encourage them with God's answers! We need to share our answers to prayers as well. It's easy to give prayer requests, but we must remember to share His answers! Why? Because sharing answers to prayer encourages others.

WHAT CAN WE LEARN FROM THIS?

Rhoda teaches us that as believers, we can experience boundless joy. Peter shows us that we can trust even in the face of persecution. Do you feel some emotional distance between yourself and other Christians? Have you faced ridicule for your stance on specific values that others may not share?

It's okay. Keep knocking. Keep on keeping on. Stay focused on Christ—not the Christians around you.

And finally . . . we learn that God is still in the business of answering prayer!

When you can't see Him move, you can always trust His heart.

The God who rescued Daniel from the lion's den, saved Shadrack, Meshach, and Abednego, answered prayers and freed Peter from prison, and prominently featured a lowly slave girl in His story is the same God who has a place for YOU in His story.

He's the same God who hears every prayer you pray, and this same God is still moving, answering, rescuing, and working in our lives . . . right now!

GOING DEEPER

- Identify a time you prayed for something specific and were surprised when God answered.
- What are some values you hold that not all Christians share?
- (Abstaining from alcohol, church attendance, etc.) How can you remain-encouraged to keep the values God has given you?
- Describe something you regularly pray for with other believers?
- Go to YouTube and listen to Hannah Kerr's song "Same God" and reflect on the faithfulness of God in your life.

SHE DIDN'T BACK DOWN. SHE EXHIBITED BOLDNESS.

THE BELIEVERS WERE POURING OUT THEIR HEARTS TO GOD ON PETER'S BEHALF.

IT WAS EASIER TO GET OUT OF PRISON THAN IT WAS TO GET INTO THIS PRAYER MEETING!

ONE-HIT WONDER:
ERNO RUBIK

What consists of 26 small, colorful cubes rotating on an axis with 43 quintillion possible configurations? You guessed it! It's the Rubik's Cube. There's only one configuration that aligns the colors correctly in its original arrangement.

Erno Rubik from Budapest, Hungary, gained popularity with this ingenious puzzle in the 1980s. Approximately 50 books have been published describing how to solve the puzzle. Though Erno created a few other puzzles, he's primarily known for the Rubik's cube, making him a one-hit wonder.

CHAPTER SIX

(1 Kings 13)

Two Prophets Out to Lunch: Part 1

Things aren't always as they appear. That's why it's crucial for Christ-followers to always follow His guidance. Failing to do so can be destructive.

Let's dive into an obscure little story tucked inside of 1 Kings 13. We'll learn a lot from this odd story in the Old Testament—beginning with these two things:

#1: How easy it is to be deceived.

#2: How important it is to know God's truth and not be moved from it.

But before we dive into the story, let's get the background from 1 Kings 12. Evil King Jeroboam is ruling Israel, and he established the worship of two golden calves and declared,

"Here are your gods, Israel,
who brought you up out of Egypt."
(Kings 12:28 NIV)

What a liar!

Yes, this was deceitful. It also wasn't very smart.

How could a golden, lifeless calf lead approximately a million Israelites anywhere? Not even a living calf could guide an exodus like that!

Have you ever seen a golden calf? I haven't. But all of us are at risk of having one... something that can easily be placed on a pedestal in our lives and suddenly dominate everything we do. By examining our own lives carefully, each of us can find something that might quickly become our "golden calf"—whether it's houses, land, children, family, recreation, entertainment, or whatever else.

Anything we allow into our lives that replaces God, *even briefly,* becomes our golden calf—the idol—that we worship. And even a moment of making that thing the center of our lives can lead us to a place of spiritual trouble and cost us much more in our walk with the Lord than we ever imagined.

COUNTERFEITS AND WARNINGS

King Jeroboam held a feast, offered incense, and burnt sacrifices—all to imitate and replace the Passover feast that God had established. In other words, this feast was a counterfeit of the Passover. Have you noticed that Satan always works through counterfeits? Consider the miracles of Moses when he pleaded with Pharaoh to release the Israelites. Pharaoh's magicians imitated those miracles.

We understand that God has established Himself in the Trinity: God, Jesus Christ, and the Holy Spirit. Satan has created a counterfeit trinity. We see this false trinity in Revelation:

Satan is the dragon,

the Anti-Christ is the Beast,

and the False Prophet is the other component.

Back to Jeroboam. He had transformed the city of Bethel into a center of idol worship. From there, he spread idol worship throughout all of Israel! The idol worship Jeroboam introduced was destroying the nation and provoking God's anger, but his stubborn heart refused to heed the warnings God sent.

So, God sent another warning—on high volume—through a prophet. We don't know this prophet's name. Scripture only refers to him as "the man of God." So let's use the first letters of those words and call him **TMOG:** **T**he **M**an **O**f **G**od.

Let's go to Scripture:

"By the word of the Lord a man of God came from Judah to Bethel, as Jeroboam was standing by the altar to make an offering." (1 Kings 13:1 NIV)

Again, the idol worship Jeroboam introduced to Israel was destroying the nation and bringing God's wrath against them, but his hard heart wouldn't listen to the warnings God sent.

"By the word of the Lord he cried out against the altar: 'Altar, altar! This is what the Lord says: 'A son named Josiah will be born to the house of David. On you he will sacrifice the priests of the high places who make offerings here, and human bones will be burned on you.' "
(1 Kings 13:1-2 NIV)

What's going on here?

TMOG delivered a genuine prophetic word that would be fulfilled about 350 years later, when a godly king named Josiah rose to power in Israel. He would burn down the idols and put an end to worshiping the Golden Calf. Let's keep reading. The story moves quickly from here!

"That same day the man of God gave a sign: 'This is the sign the Lord has declared: The altar will be split apart and the ashes on it will be poured out.' "
(1 Kings 13:3 NIV)

King Jeroboam didn't want his altars torn apart. So, he reacted in anger:

"The king was very angry with the prophet for saying this. He shouted to his guards, 'Arrest that man!' and shook his fist at him. Instantly the king's arm became paralyzed in that position; he couldn't pull it back again!
"At the same moment a wide crack appeared in the altar and the ashes poured out, just as the prophet had said would happen.
"For this was the prophet's proof that God had been speaking through him."
(1 Kings 13:4-5 TLB)

When Jeroboam reached out to grab TMOG, God shriveled and paralyzed the king's hand.

" 'Oh, please, please,' the king cried out to the prophet, 'beg the Lord your God to restore my arm again.'
"So he prayed to the Lord, and the king's arm became normal again."
(1 Kings 13:6 TLB)

God's presence was so powerful with TMOG, He gave him healing power to restore Jeroboam's arm.

But look closely. There was no sign of repentance from King Jeroboam. Notice that *he* didn't pray—

he didn't ask God to forgive him. Instead, he asked TMOG to pray!

He wasn't willing to repent—or he would have prayed himself. There was no remorse for the sin of idol-worship he led the people of Israel into. He just wanted his arm back!

Let's keep reading:

**"Then the king said to the prophet,
'Come to the palace with me and rest
awhile and have some food;
and I'll give you a reward because
you healed my arm.'"
(1 Kings 13:7 TLB)**

Because the king couldn't force TMOG, he's now trying to win him over with kindness and wealth.

If Satan can't beat us, he'll try to buy us!

But TMOG demonstrated amazing restraint.

Here it is:

**"But the man of God answered the king,
'Even if you were to give me half your
possessions, I would not go with you, nor
would I eat bread or drink water here.
" 'For I was commanded by the word of
the Lord: 'You must not eat bread or drink
water or return by the way you came.'
"So he took another road and did not
return by the way he had come to Bethel."
(1 Kings 13:8-10 NIV)**

God was specific with this prophet.

Go tell King Jeroboam this specific message I have given you.

When you're finished, don't eat or drink, and go home a different route.

GOD'S CHARACTER

We serve a God of specifics.

He doesn't deal in generalities.

The first thing He did after creating Adam—even before forming Eve out of Adam's rib—was to give Adam a specific warning.

"The Lord God took the man and put him in the Garden of Eden to work it and take care of it. And the Lord God commanded the man, 'You are free to eat from any tree in the garden; but you must not eat form the tree of the knowledge of good and evil, for when you eat of it you will surely die.' "
(Genesis 2:15-17 NIV)

Notice how specific God was?

Adam knew where the tree was located.

He knew exactly which tree it was.

And he knew precisely what not to do with the tree.

We serve a God who is never cryptic when giving a warning. God has never made an empty threat. He does what He says. And He has given specific instructions to TMOG:

- Go to Bethel, the city of idols.
- Confront King Jeroboam.
- Prophesy about the altar.
- Leave the city of Bethel.
- Don't eat or drink anything.

TMOG was obedient. We see him living in God's will.

It's safe to say he was exhausted from his journey—and no doubt thirsty and hungry—yet ~~but~~ he refused the King's offer! No amount of money would turn TMOG away from the Lord. He was demonstrating radical obedience to God's instructions. What a test that was, but he passed with flying colors.

So far, the Lord had blessed him with a dynamic ministry. Amazing things were happening. But often—after a spiritual victory—Satan will try his best to discourage us.

Remember the story of Elijah and the prophets of Baal? (Check out 1 Kings 18 and 19). After Elijah called fire down from heaven, burned a bull without matches or kerosene and defeated 450 prophets of Baal, he hid in a cave and told God he wanted to die. *What?!?*

He was focusing on Queen Jezebel's threat to kill him instead of celebrating the great victory God had just given him. You see, Satan knows your weak spot, and he understands what it takes to lead you astray from the path God has set before you.

Satan will make the temptation seem so innocent.
So necessary.
So right.
But the end of that path leads to total disaster.

**"There is a way that appears to be right,
but in the end it leads to death."
(Proverbs 14:12 NIV)**

Satan will make the road look right,
feel right
and seem right.
He is a master at making disobedience make sense.
Again, the end of the path leads to total disaster.
In fact, it can lead to losing your family

your ministry

your job

your friends

your reputation

your home

your life.

Only you and God know if you're on the right path.

Right now (yes, while you're reading this chapter), is a perfect moment to examine your heart. Right here. Right now.

Will you ask God to show you in the next few minutes if you're heading down the wrong path?

WHAT SATAN HATES

Satan despises it when you follow God. He won't just sit back and let you walk into heaven without resisting. You can be sure he knows who you are, and Satan will do everything he can to stop you as you try to serve the Lord.

Often, it's a small thing that seems so innocent that distracts us. But the small detour from the straight and narrow can take us much farther than we ever expected, sometimes even ending our ministry . . . or marriage.

Entire ministries have entered a self-destructive phase because of one minister's failure who fell into the devil's trap. The devil knew his weakness and deliberately set a trap in his way.

Satan is keenly aware of your weaknesses and will do everything he can to trip you up! Don't let him. Stay alert, as the apostle Peter encourages us to do:

"Be careful—watch out for attacks from Satan, your great enemy. He prowls around like a hungry, roaring lion, looking for some victim to tear apart. Stand firm when he attacks. Trust the Lord. . . ."
(1 Peter 5:8-9 TLB)

Satan also knows what you value most. If you greatly cherish family, do you really think he'll stay away from this part of your life?

a. Not sure.

b. I hope so.

c. Probably not.

d. Never thought about it.

(The answer is NO!) He'll try to undermine you or a family member. How many pastors do you know who loved and cherished their families? Yet they still crossed inappropriate boundaries with someone of the opposite sex and ended up losing what they valued most.

I was speaking at a pastor's retreat when their district leader shared a story about having to revoke the credentials of one of his pastors. He said, "Susie, he was a great preacher. Articulate, dynamic, young, exciting. But he crossed the line. Went too far with a female in his congregation. When I met with him, he broke down and wept. 'I knew it was wrong,' he said. 'I just let my guard down.' It broke my heart. But I couldn't allow him to continue in ministry. That one mistake cost him his calling."

We must always be on guard lest something or someone tries to lead us astray.

Let's check out what Paul asked the Galatians:

"You were running the race so well.
Who has held you back from
following the truth?"
(Galatians 5:7 NLT)

Something to chew on, isn't it?

BACK TO THE STORY

So far, we've seen TMOG make wise decisions. He's following God's authority with complete dedication! But now Satan will try to stop him. Satan has set a trap—one that would be difficult to see until it's too late. Satan is always trying and never gives up. Once again, we must stay alert!

TMOG was in God's will, doing God's work, and had a very promising future as a true Prophet of God. But as he walked along, the excitement of the moment and the power of God's move began to fade into the past.

He was weary, hungry, and thirsty, so he found a place to rest. Now, there's nothing wrong with resting—unless we rest too long—and in the wrong place! Let's keep reading:

"Now there was a certain old prophet living in Bethel." (1 Kings 13:11 NIV)

Notice, we're not given his name. All we know is that he's an old prophet of God. So let's call him **OPOG: O**ld **P**rophet **O**f **G**od.

Okay, we've all been tricked—especially on April Fool's Day. A guy I used to work with placed a dead mouse in a co-worker's desk drawer on April 1. *Ewww.*

A friend of mine found the keys to a woman's car who worked in our office and moved her vehicle to a completely different part of the parking lot. It took her a long time to find it.

Unlike humorous April Fool's tricks, however, Satan's tricks aren't funny. They're malicious,

deceptive,

and have eternal consequences.

In this Bible account, Satan is about to reach into his evil bag of tricks and try a quick move on TMOG. The enemy found an old prophet—OPOG—who lived in Bethel, where Jeroboam's idol worship was strong.

OPOG may have been a man of God once, but he lived among the sin of idolatry for too long and had become accustomed to it—even tolerating it—never speaking out against it.

He had found his comfort zone and decided to stay.

OPOG knew idolatry was wrong.

And sure—he still knew about God, and maybe he still worshipped God once in a while. But he had *lost the anointing* God had given him as a prophet.

Every now and then, he'd feel God, and that was enough for him.

He had seriously deteriorated spiritually, and that didn't bother him at all.

OPOG didn't care that he wasn't living in God's will! If fact, he was completely *out* of God's will by choosing to live in sin city and accepting the sin around him.

Tolerance isn't always a good thing.

TWO PROPHETS MEET

As we continue reading, we find OPOG approaching TMOG.

". . . he found him sitting under an oak tree and asked, 'Are you the man of God who came from Judah?'
" 'I am,' he replied."
(1 Kings 13:11-14 NIV)

The term used here is "sitting" under the oak tree. But in this context, sitting means much more than just sitting in the shade and taking a break. TMOG had actually established a temporary home and was living under that oak tree. He had built a shelter for himself. How long had he been there? A few weeks? A couple of months?

TMOG's first mistake was not leaving the land of idolatry. God had told him to move on—to go home a different way—but TMOG decided to rest for a while... and he rested too long and in the wrong place!

Now Satan sprung his trap, and he used an old, spiritually deteriorated prophet of God to do the work for him.

Let's watch as Satan's plan unfolds before our eyes:

"Then the old man said to the prophet, 'Come home with me and eat.'
" 'No,' he replied. 'I can't; for I am not allowed to eat anything or to drink any water at Bethel. The Lord strictly warned me against it; and he also told me not to

return home by the same road I came on.'
"But the old man said, 'I am a prophet too,
just as you are; and an angel
gave me a message from the Lord.
I am to take you home with me and give
you food and water.'
"But the old man was lying to him.
So they went back together, and the
prophet ate some food and drank some
water at the old man's home."
(1 Kings 13:15-19 TLB)

Be cautious when someone approaches you saying, "I have a word for you." We must ensure that the word is truly from the Lord and not from the heart of another Christian with his own hidden agenda for giving you a word.

Too many people have let a "word" spoken by someone else lead them away from the will of God. And just like this old prophet, the word given is still a lie, even if it was given with good intentions.

'I am a prophet too, just as you are.' . . .

Maybe this was true sometime in the past, but this old man was only a shadow of what he used to be—because if he had been a prophet like the young man was—someone God could rely on to deliver the message—then there wouldn't have been a need to send someone from Judah to Bethel.

How had this OPOG gotten to this point?

He was a prophet who lived in Bethel.

He lived in the realm of rebellion.

He had a personal knowledge of Jeroboam's ways.

He saw the golden image he had made to worship, and he'd seen the altar erected, but he hadn't done anything about it!

He was ignoring his job description as prophet!

OPOG's sin is negligence.

It's the sin of doing nothing!

It's also the sin of tolerance.

It's the sin of neutrality!

God had to find a man from Judah (TMOG) to do the job because OPOG wasn't doing it! We all want to be used by God, but if we're not obedient, He'll find someone else to carry out the task. Grab a sandwich and a glass of lemonade, and we'll dive into part two of this story in the next chapter.

GOING DEEPER:

- **What are some common examples of modern idols? Do you have any "golden calves" that are coming between you and God? Anything that you're investing too much time, energy and focus on can be an idol.**
- **Are you on the right path? Or have you possibly been lured onto a path that *seems* right and looks enticing but is actually leading you toward disaster?**
- **Have you truly repented? King Jeroboam never repented. He stood next to God's true prophet—heard God's voice through the prophet—even experienced a miracle from God—yet never really knew God.**

Repentance is different than confession. Repentance is walking away from a sinful lifestyle. Confession is asking God to forgive your sins. Many of us stop short after confession and never repent. Is it possible that you've asked God for forgiveness but are still holding onto a sinful part of your life?

Before you move into Part Two of ***Two Prophets Out to Lunch***, absorb this:

How much sin does God wink at?
a. We can scoot by with *some* sin.
b. It depends on the situation.
c. No one really knows.
d. God never winks at sin.

The correct answer is NONE. God never winks at sin. All sin must be judged. Because of TMOG's disobedience to follow the express will of God and not turn aside to eat or drink or get off of the path that God had directed him to walk, TMOG will experience grave consequences.

His ministry will soon cease.

Does this seem harsh?

We have to remember that God isn't playing games. Though He is long-suffering, there will come a point when He won't tolerate sin and disobedience any longer.

So when does God's patience run out?

Only God knows!

It's a chance we can't afford to take!

What should we do?

We should ask God to search our hearts.

"Search me, God, and know my heart;
test me and know my anxious thoughts.
See if there is any offensive way in me,
and lead me in the way everlasting."
(Psalm 139:23-24 NIV)

The Word of God doesn't change.

Man may alter it,

lie about it,

and add to it,

but God's Word will endure forever.

CHAPTER SEVEN

(1 Kings 13)

Two Prophets Out to Lunch: Part 2

Because there wasn't enough space to include this story in just one chapter, keep reading about two guys with a heartbreaking tale.

We're talking about an obscure little story tucked inside of 1 Kings 13 and it clearly shows us these two truths:

#1: How easy it is to be deceived.

#2: How important it is to know God's truth and not be moved from it.

Let's recap our characters:

- **Wicked King Jeroboam** (Idol worship)
- **The Man Of God: TMOG** (Prophet from Judah)
- **Old Prophet Of God: OPOG** (God's former prophet who lived in Bethel, Israel)

"By the word of the Lord a man of God came from Judah to Bethel, as Jeroboam was standing by the altar to make an offering.

By the word of the Lord he cried out against the altar: 'Altar, altar! This is what the Lord says: "A son named Josiah will be born to the house of David. On you he will sacrifice the priests of the high places who make offerings here, and human bones will be burned on you." ' That same day the man of God gave a sign: This is the sign the Lord has declared: ' The altar will be split apart and the ashes on it will be poured out.

"The king was very angry with the prophet for saying this. He shouted to his guards, 'Arrest that man!' and shook his fist at him.

"Instantly the king's arm became paralyzed in that position; he couldn't pull it back again!

"At the same moment a wide crack appeared in the altar and the ashes poured out, just as the prophet had said would happen.

"For this was the prophet's proof that God had been speaking through him. 'Oh, please, please,' the king cried out to the prophet, 'beg the Lord your God to restore my arm again.'

"So he prayed to the Lord, and the king's arm became normal again.
"Then the king said to the prophet, 'Come to the palace with me and rest awhile and have some food; and I'll give you a reward because you healed my arm.'
"But the man of God answered the king, 'Even if you were to give me half your possessions, I would not go with you, nor would I eat bread or drink water here. For I was commanded by the word of the Lord: 'You must not eat bread or drink water or return by the way you came.'
"So he took another road and did not return by the way he had come to Bethel."
(1 Kings 13:1-10 NIV)

Let's remember from our previous chapter: TMOG is exhausted from his journey. He's thirsty and hungry, but he refuses the king's offer! That was a huge test, but he passed with flying colors.

WHAT SATAN HATES

Satan hates it when you obey God. He's not going to sit by and let you walk into heaven without resistance. Satan will do everything he can to stop you on your journey through life as you try to serve the Lord.

Entire ministries have fallen into a self-destructive mode because of the failure of one minister who was lured into the devil's trap. The devil knew exactly what it would take to cause him to stumble; and that's what was placed in his path. Satan is acutely aware of your weak spots, and he'll do everything in his power to trip you up!

Let's keep following the story:

"Quick, saddle the donkey,"
the old man said. And when they had
saddled the donkey for him, he rode
after the prophet and found him
sitting under an oak tree.
"Are you the prophet who came
from Judah?" he asked him.
" 'I am,' he replied.
"Then the old man said to the prophet,
'Come home with me and eat.'
" 'No,' he replied. 'I can't; for I am not
allowed to eat anything or to drink any
water at Bethel. The Lord strictly warned
me against it; and he also told me not to
return home by the same road I came on.'
"But the old man said, 'I am a
prophet too, just as you are; and
an angel gave me a message from the
Lord. I am to take you home with me
and give you food and water.'
"But the old man was lying to him. So
they went back together, and the prophet
[TMOG] ate some food and drank some
water at the old man's home."
(1 Kings 13:11-19 TLB)

TMOG knew what was right . . . but he wasn't doing it.

You, too, probably know what's right.

Are you doing it?

We can know God's will without living inside of His will, and this is a dangerous place for a Christian to be.

There's no indication that OPOG intended to harm TMOG. He only wanted his company for a while. He probably admired the courage TMOG showed in confronting the king and the boldness to speak out against idolatry. But even if his reasons were good, his methods were entirely wrong. OPOG used lies and manipulation to steer TMOG away from God's perfect will.

And what about TMOG?

Shouldn't he have been able to see what was happening?

Why did he follow the old prophet when he already had God's instructions and knew what he should be doing?

TMOG had heard from God Himself.

OPOG had simply heard from an angel.

Which was better?

Perhaps TMOG thought, *Well, this is a prophet of God too. Maybe God is guiding me in a different direction for a while. What could be so wrong about hearing what my fellow prophet has to say?*

THE DANGER OF DISOBEDIENCE

The apostle Paul, many years later, would write these sobering words to the church:

"I am amazed that you are turning away so soon from God who, in his love and mercy, invited you to share the eternal life he gives through Christ; you are already following a different 'way to heaven,' which really doesn't go to heaven at all. "For there is no other way than the one we showed you; you are being fooled by those who twist and change the truth concerning Christ. "Let God's curses fall on anyone, including myself, who preaches any other way to be saved than the one we told you about; yes, if an angel comes from heaven and preaches any other message, let him be forever cursed." (Galatians 1:6-8 TLB)

Just because something we hear sounds like the truth, doesn't mean it is. Satan often uses a little truth hidden inside his pack of lies. TMOG fell into the trap and went home with the old prophet. They had a great visit and enjoyed being together for a while.

But then God entered the scene, and everything changed. Let's turn back to Scripture:

"Then, suddenly, while they were sitting at the table, a message from the Lord came to the old man, and he shouted at the

prophet from Judah, 'The Lord says that because you have been disobedient to his clear command and have come here, and have eaten and drunk water in the place he told you not to, therefore your body shall not be buried in the grave of your fathers.'

"After finishing the meal, the old man saddled the prophet's donkey, and the prophet started off again. But as he was traveling along, a lion came out and killed him.

"His body lay there on the road, with the donkey and the lion standing beside it. Those who came by and saw the body lying in the road and the lion standing quietly beside it, reported it in Bethel where the old prophet lived."

(1 Kings 13:19-25 TLB)

Whaaaat???

God followed through on the consequence He promised.

God has never made an empty threat.

There *are* times in Scripture when He changes His mind, but in each of those cases, either intercession or repentance (Jonah 3:10) was involved—both of which are part of His plan for dealing with mankind.

You may be familiar with the intercession situation in Exodus 32:14. The children of Israel made a golden calf from their jewelry and metal possessions while Moses was on the mountain with God; and God said He'd bring disaster on them as soon as Moses came down from the mountain.

But Moses prayed for them, interceded for them, begged God's mercy on them, and God relented. But He has never once given a hollow warning.

Okay, but hold on a minute. If OPOG wasn't living in God's will, how could he give TMOG a true word from the Lord?

God often uses nonbelievers to fulfill His will, implement His plan, or help bring His children back into a relationship with Him. For instance, God used the Midianites (see Judges 6:1-14) to oppress the Israelites until they realized they had strayed from God and needed to realign themselves with righteousness.

In fact, this is a cycle in the Old Testament. We see God's people loving and serving Him, then they get comfortable. They let down their guard, worship idols, and before long, they're no longer serving God. That's when God uses nonbelievers to wake up His children. The Israelites (His children) then return to loving and serving Him, but they get comfortable again, let down their guard, worship idols, and stop serving God. This cycle repeats again and again.

In the story we're currently in, we see God using an old, dried-up former prophet of God—who's no longer serving Him—to deliver a word of truth to TMOG.

Let's continue the story:

"His body lay there on the road,
with the donkey and the lion standing
beside it. Those who came by and saw
the body lying in the road and the lion
standing quietly beside it, reported it in
Bethel where the old prophet lived.
"When he heard what had happened
he exclaimed, 'It is the prophet who
disobeyed the Lord's command;
the Lord fulfilled his warning by causing
the lion to kill him.'
"Then he said to his sons, 'Saddle
my donkey!' And they did.
"He found the prophet's body lying in
the road; and the donkey and lion were
still standing there beside it,
for the lion had not eaten the body
nor attacked the donkey.
"So the prophet laid the body upon the
donkey and took it back to the city to
mourn over it and bury it.
"Afterwards he said to his sons,
'When I die, bury me in the grave where
the prophet is buried. Lay my bones
beside his bones.' "
(1 Kings 13:24-31 TLB)

SPIRITUAL DETERIORATION

OPOG had spiritually deteriorated, but he still wanted to be close to someone spiritual, so he asked to be buried next to TMOG. This gives us more insight into OPOG. He probably wasn't very mature spiritually, or he would have known that simply being *next* to someone spiritual wouldn't make *him* spiritual.

You'd think he would've known that he could repent and return to spiritual alignment with God. Yes, OPOG could have turned back to God. But because he had lived in sin city for so long—ignoring God's voice for so long—he stopped caring about things of the Lord.

Now he's so spiritually confused, he unfortunately thinks being buried next to TMOG will somehow work in his favor.

Let's continue with the story in Scripture:

**"Despite the prophet's warning,
Jeroboam did not turn away from his
evil ways; instead, he made more priests
than ever from the common people,
to offer sacrifices to idols in the
shrines on the hills.
"Anyone who wanted to could be a priest.
This was a great sin and resulted in the
destruction of Jeroboam's kingdom and
the death of all of his family."
(1 Kings 13:33 TLB)**

What a sad story.

Jeroboam's kingdom collapses.

He and his family die.

TMOG loses his ministry and his life.

And OPOG ends up in the same grave!

Before we wrap up this story, let's focus for a moment on TMOG's major flaw: He didn't know *a conflicting message to God's word, cannot also be from God.*

That's seriously important to remember.

In fact, there are a few seriously important things to remember from this story. Let's look at them:

#1: GOD'S WORD IS FOREVER SETTLED.

It does NOT change. Today, if a message from a dream, vision, prophecy, experience, testimony, feeling, Book of Mormon, Koran, or anything else contradicts or conflicts with the Bible, we must reject it.

TMOG was very sincere, but he made the mistake of believing the wrong message that he was told was from God.

We must be guarded and *stick like glue* to the message of the Bible.

Don't let anyone or anything pull you away from God's Word—even someone you love deeply.

If you get distracted, you might be deceived, and deception can be deadly. We are fighting for eternity. Stay very cautious and test everything.

What are we told in the last book of the Bible?

"I am coming soon. Hold on to what you have, so that no one will take your crown." (Revelation 3:11 NIV)

#2: SIN WILL NOT BE TOLERATED.

Whether it's sin from a hard-hearted, backslidden king or a Christian who chooses even for a moment to step outside of God's will, sin's cost is heavy—too heavy to bear—as its price is always death.

TMOG's life and ministry were over.

What should we do?

We should examine our actions.

"Then why should we, mere humans, complain when we are punished for our sins? Instead, let us test and examine our ways. Let us turn back to the Lord." (Lamentations 3:39-40 NLT)

#3: KNOW GOD'S VOICE AND OBEY IT.

TMOG heard God's voice and knew His will. However, he allowed another voice to drown out God's. Just because a Christian speaks God's Word doesn't mean they are living in God's will. Be discerning!

When God gives you clear direction and you know the way you should go, WALK IN IT! If you listen to others, be absolutely sure that the words you hear *only confirm* what you already know from God Himself and His written Word. God never contradicts Himself. Don't let even well-meaning Christians steer you away from the path God has chosen for your life.

TMOG knew for sure what God had told him. He *wasn't* certain what God had said to the old prophet—or if God had spoken to the old prophet at all.

A word from an angel never trumps a word from God Himself. And remember . . . there are several fallen angels acting as Satan's mouthpieces to deceive Christians.

#4: GOD IS LOVE, FORGIVENESS, JUSTICE, HOLINESS, JUDGMENT, AND MERCY.

God still loved TMOG—even though He allowed the lion to kill him.

We've read in Scripture that when OPOG went to get TMOG's body and bring it back to bury him, the lion was still there, and the donkey stood right there, both of them never leaving TMOG's dead body until the old prophet came to retrieve it.

God still loved TMOG. Even though he was disobedient and faced judgment and death for his sin, God continued to watch over his body and protect it for burial.

It must have been the Lord's presence that kept the lion from devouring what he had killed and allowed the donkey to stand there with the lion, unafraid until help arrived.

I believe, after seeing how God cared even for TMOG's dead body, that God ultimately saved his soul. I trust TMOG knew God well enough not to fail to repent at the last minute.

I believe that when the lion was attacking him, TMOG was pleading for God's forgiveness. And God will always forgive a truly repentant heart.

But oh, how much was lost!

#5: DON'T SACRIFICE WHAT GOD WANTS TO DO WITH YOUR LIFE FOR TEMPORARY PLEASURE!

TMOG had experienced the incredible presence and power of God. He had been used to bring signs and wonders from heaven. He was a true man of God and a great prophet—but now his ministry and his life were finished—because of the fleeting pleasure of being tempted by OPOG and sharing food and drink with him.

HOW MUCH WAS LOST?

How much had TMOG lost through one act of disobedience? How much more could he have experienced or achieved in a lifetime of ministry if only he'd fully obeyed God?

Maybe he would've had another fifty years of incredible ministry! Perhaps he would've been included in the hall of faith in Hebrews 11.

Maybe we would have known his name! And maybe in Sunday school or Bible studies, we'd be learning about the ongoing miracles God performed through him. But because he was disobedient and allowed himself to fall into the trap of deception, this is all we have—an obscure little story about a man with no name.

What about you? Are you walking in God's will, following the call He has placed on your life, and being faithful before Him? Have you been tempted away by Satan's tricks?

GOING DEEPER:

- **Think of something that could grab your attention, draw you away from God's perfect path, and entice you to follow after something that seems more important?**
- **How might the above lead you to a place where you don't even realize how far you've strayed from God's will?**
- **How do we wander so far that we risk losing the very things we cherish most—family, ministering to others, truly loving and serving God?**

God has never made an empty threat.

We can know God's will without living inside of His will.

A conflicting message to God's Word cannot also be from God.

ONE-HIT WONDER: BOBBY PICKETT

Monster MASH

Buckle your seatbelts! We're traveling back in time to 1962. The BBC banned the song "Monster Mash" in the United Kingdom because they thought it was too morbid. It still became a hit in the U.S., and it's often played around Halloween. But Bobby Pickett? He didn't do anything noteworthy afterward. He was a one-hit wonder.

CHAPTER EIGHT

(Judges 5:24-27)

She Nailed It!

Did she belong to a Girl Scout group when she was young? Did she excel in martial arts? Was she a champion sword fighter? No. But Jael definitely had a solid strategy for taking out the enemy.

"Most blessed among women is Jael, the wife of Heber the Kenite.

May she be blessed above all women who live in tents.

"Sisera asked for water, and she gave him milk. In a bowl fit for nobles, she brought him yogurt. Then with her left hand she reached for a tent peg, and with her right hand for the workman's hammer.

She struck Sisera with the hammer,
crushing his head. With a shattering blow,
she pierced his temples.
"He sank, he fell, he lay still at her feet.
And where he sank, there he died."
(Judges 5:24-27 NLT)

Victory was achieved, and it was time to celebrate! Judges 5 features a hymn sung by Deborah, an Israelite judge, and Barak, the military leader. This hymn is one of the oldest parts of the Bible. It occurred during an early period of Israelite history, when there was no king. Instead, Israel was organized as a loose confederation of twelve tribes, led by a judge who served as both a military and spiritual leader.

The period of the judges lasted roughly from 1400 to 1000 BC. Deborah served as a judge for about forty years, traditionally from 1107 BC to 1067 BC.

With God's help, victory was achieved over the Canaanites, and she sang a song praising the tribes that fought willingly while condemning those who stayed home and did not join the battle.

The song emphasizes leadership, highlighting the importance of committed leaders and people who dedicate themselves to God's cause, just as she did when hope seemed lost. Then, we hear special praise for Jael, the woman who killed Sisera. You read correctly—the *woman* who brought the conflict to an end by killing Sisera. It's hard to fully appreciate the victory without understanding the struggle that preceded it. Let's go back and meet Jael.

A Little Bit of Background

Jael [JAY-uhl] means "mountain goat," representing a climber. It fits our heroine who saved Israel from the Canaanite forces led by King Hazor and General Sisera.

She was an ordinary woman with no special distinction.

She is briefly introduced in Judges 4:

"Sisera, meanwhile, fled on foot to the tent of Jael, the wife of Heber the Kenite . . . "
(Judges 4:17 NIV)

That's all. She's described in just four words: the wife of Heber. Her identity was defined by her marriage. She was unknown. She wasn't a matriarch of faith like Sarah; she wasn't a queen like Esther. Neither was she known as a prophet like Miriam, nor a judge like Deborah. She was simply Jael, the wife of Heber. God used her to fulfill His purposes. She rose from obscurity to make her mark in Jewish history, so never underestimate the power of an ordinary woman willing to be used by God!

She grew up during a time of great hardship. For twenty years, the Israelites endured oppression under Canaanite King Jabin's rule, whose army was led by the feared General Sisera. There were 900 iron chariots under his command. That was both impressive and intimidating, providing a strong military advantage against any opposing force.

During twenty years of oppression, God's people endured great suffering. Because of Sisera's powerful army, the Canaanites managed to impose an economic blockade, preventing any buying or selling. This caused a forced (or artificial) famine for Israel, created by their enemies to push them toward despair. Along with the famine, there were also raids on towns. During these attacks, the Canaanite army stole goods, plundered villages, and men took women and girls into slavery of all kinds. This went on for twenty years, but eventually Israel called upon the Lord.

Let's pause for a moment and think about that last sentence: "eventually Israel called upon the Lord." That's staggering. It's hard to believe. It's sad.

You might think that would've been their immediate response. Would it be yours? I hope so! Instead, Israel waited two decades to do anything! This period of oppression stemmed from their ongoing idolatry and disobedience.

When God's people choose to do things their own way instead of His, it always leads to oppression and trouble. We've all faced similar situations at some point. That's where they were, and after all those long, hard years, they yearned for something different. So, they cried out to God,

". . . then the people of Israel cried out to the LORD for help." (Judges 4:3 NLT)

And God heard their cry.

SETTING THE STAGE: A MOTHER IN ISRAEL

**"Deborah, the wife of Lappidoth,
was a prophet who was
judging Israel at that time."
(Judges 4:4 NLT)**

Deborah was the fourth judge of Israel and the only woman judge mentioned in the Bible. She was also a wife and a prophetess of God to her people. As a judge, her responsibilities were similar to those of judges today—leading and resolving legal disputes. She also took on military duties as part of her role.

Being a prophet meant she was responsible not only for guiding the tribes of Israel but also for acting as God's spokesperson, declaring, "Thus sayeth the LORD!" to the people. In that role, she exercised spiritual discernment, hearing God's voice and delivering His messages with authority. That authority is clear in our story today.

**"She would sit under the Palm
of Deborah, between Ramah and Bethel
in the hill country of Ephraim,
and the Israelites would go to her for
judgment. One day, she sent for Barak
son of Abinoam, who lived in
Kedesh in Naphtali . . . "
(Judges 4:5-6 NLT)**

During her leadership, Israel appeared to go through an emotional rollercoaster with their dedication to God. Their shifting actions revealed their fundamental struggle: selfishness and sin. Remember, this is what led to their twenty-year hardship. Each day, Deborah sat beneath her favorite palm tree, judging her people's conduct much the way a mother cares for her children. The Bible doesn't specify if she had children, but it shows she was a spiritual mother, guiding those entrusted to her. This is what we're told:

"There were few people left in the villages of Israel—until Deborah arose as a mother for Israel." (Judges 5:7 NLT)

We see this dedication and care in leadership when God gave her a specific message to deliver to her military leader.

Moved by her people's suffering and God's urgent call, she summoned the Israelite military commander, Barak, from the tribe of Naphtali, and gave these instructions:

"This is what the LORD, the God of Israel, commands you: Call out 10,000 warriors from the tribes of Naphtali and Zebulun at Mount Tabor. And I will call out Sisera, commander of Jabin's army, along with his chariots and warriors, to the Kishon River. There I will give you victory over him." (Judges 4:6-7 NLT)

Do you remember earlier in Judges 4:3 when God's people cried out to Him for help? Here's proof that He listened and responded. His answer was to grant victory over the Canaanite army, Sisera, and King Jabin, along with the 900 iron chariots. That was the message from God's prophet to Barak. All Barak had to do was go, and he would be the victorious military leader, the hero of the story. God said it, and His word is certain; victory will come. You can trust it: Just go with the army to the Kishon River and watch God work! But

"Barak said, "If you go with me, I'll go. But if you don't go with me, I won't go." (Judges 4:8 The Message)

Wait, what?

We need to pause and talk.

It was truly exhilarating to realize that after twenty years of suffering, God had a plan to save His people. They finally cried out, and God responded. He spoke through His prophet to the would-be hero of the story—the military leader of God's army. All he needed to do was go, but he said no.

How would you respond to that? I know I'd probably wish the fate of Jonah on him. I guess twenty years weren't enough, so maybe a few days in the belly of a big fish would change his mind. Or, if I were Deborah, I'd be tempted to call down fire from heaven to get him to move. And I mean quickly!

God's about to bring victory, and you're wimping out? Barak, can't you just do what God is telling you to do? Why is it that you need someone to hold your hand? I mean, if the Creator of the universe's hand isn't big enough, what hand would be? Come on, dude. Go! Again, I ask, how would you respond? Like me? Or, like Deborah?

"She said, 'Of course I'll go with you. But understand that with an attitude like that, there'll be no glory in it for you. GOD will use a woman's hand to take care of Sisera.' " (Judges 4:9 The Message)

The stage was set for Barak to be used powerfully by God and to become a hero for His people, but he wouldn't go without Deborah. Her response was not to call Shamu or to call down fire; instead, she responded with loyalty and a desire to serve God and His people: in humility, she chose to go. She demonstrated her unwavering faith and determination but also made it clear that Barak wouldn't receive the glory. The would-be hero would no longer be a hero. Instead, God had something incredible planned. Let's look at the verse again:

"She said, 'Of course I'll go with you. But understand that with an attitude like that, there'll be no glory in it for you. God will use a woman's hand to take care of Sisera.'" (Judges 4:9-10 The Message)

GET READY TO RUMBLE

All the pieces of the puzzle were falling into place for the battle to begin, so Barak and Deborah traveled to Kedesh.

"There Barak summoned Zebulun and Naphtali, and ten thousand men went up under his command. Deborah also went up with him." (Judges 4:10 NIV)

When Sisera learned that Barak had gone up to Mount Tabor, here's what he did: "Sisera summoned from Harosheth Haggoyim to the Kishon River all his men and his nine hundred chariots fitted with iron." (Judges 4:13 NIV)

As we continue to read this passage, we see the story building to a climactic moment: God's army facing King Jabin's forces on the battlefield. However, I've skipped a verse that feels out of place or out of order. Yet, that verse offers key insight into what will happen later—the story's climax. **Here's what it says:**

"Now Heber the Kenite, a descendant of Moses' brother-in-law Hobab, had moved away from the other members of his tribe and pitched his tent by the oak of Zaanannim near Kedesh." (Judges 4:11 NLT)

Though it seems unrelated, nothing in God's Word is accidental. Why is this important? Let's step away from the battle to examine this verse.

During God's deliverance of His people from King Jabin and Sisera, the author of Judges introduces Heber the Kenite, seemingly unexpectedly. Who exactly were the Kenites? They descended from Moses' father-in-law and had settled among the Judahites, eventually becoming part of Israel (see Judges 1:6).

One of them was Heber. It's noted that he had previously left the Judahites, members of his tribe, in the south before the conflict between Barak and the Canaanites and had chosen to settle in the northern part of the Promised Land.

What's the big deal?

The only reason we know about Heber is that he's married to Jael. It seems he may have compromised himself because we read that

"Jabin king of Hazor and Heber the Kenite were on good terms with one another." (Judges 4:17 The Message)

While the rest of his people were at odds with their oppressor, Heber was at peace with him. In other words, he wasn't joining with the other Israelites to stand against the enemy persecuting them. Despite the Kenites' alliance with Israel, Heber had made peace with the Canaanite king, turning his territory into a safe haven or refuge for Jabin's forces. It seems that Heber was straddling the fence and playing both sides. And doing so is very risky. My dad used to say, "the only thing that happens when you straddle the fence is you get a hole in your britches!"

Though amusing, this highlights a serious issue. Jesus also warns against serving two masters (see Matthew 6:24), and Revelation 3:16 cautions us about being lukewarm—neither hot nor cold. The Bible repeatedly warns against these middle-ground stances. In addition to the references I mentioned, consider 1 Kings 18:21, Luke 9:62, Luke 11:23,

1 John 2:15, Joshua 24:15, James 1:8, and others that stress the dangers of divided loyalty.

Being friends with both God and His enemies—like the world or false gods—is unacceptable and threatens your spiritual health. This was how Heber was living, and as he prepared for battle, his duplicity was revealed for all to see.

BACK TO BATTLE

"Deborah said to Barak, 'Charge! This very day GOD has given you victory over Sisera. Isn't GOD marching before you?' Barak charged down the slopes of Mount Tabor, his ten companies following him. God routed Sisera—all those chariots, all those troops!—before Barak. Sisera jumped out of his chariot and ran. Barak chased the chariots and troops all the way to Harosheth Haggoyim. Sisera's entire fighting force was killed—not one man left."
(Judges 4:14-16 The Message)

Deborah's words beneath her palm tree proved true. She had received and delivered a message from God, trusting it when she asked,

"Hasn't the Lord, the God of Israel,
commanded you . . ."
(Judges 4:6 HCSB)

While Barak faced fear and doubt, she remained steadfast. She knew that 900 iron chariots were no match for God. Jabin had ruled for twenty years through constant terror, unafraid of the consequences. Though the task was intimidating (following God often is) the Lord's promise to Barak was that he would win and that he had already defeated this seemingly unstoppable enemy because God had gone ahead of him (Judges 4:14).

The stars fought from the heavens (Judges 5:20); at the River Kishon, rain (Judges 5:4) and floods (Judges 5:21) overwhelmed Sisera's forces, leading to the slaughter of the Canaanite army. When God is with you, all of nature and the universe itself support you. God directed those forces, both visible and invisible, to bring about victory! Yet Sisera seemed to escape on foot. But remember Deborah's words:

" . . . God will use a woman's hand to
take care of Sisera."
(Judges 4:9 The Message)

WATCH OUT . . . HERE SHE COMES

"Meanwhile Sisera, running for his life, headed for the tent of Jael, wife of Heber the Kenite. Jabin King of Hazor and Heber the Kenite were on good terms with one another. Jael stepped out to meet Sisera and said, 'Come in, sir. Stay here with me. Don't be afraid.' So he went with her into his tent. She covered him with a blanket. He said to her, 'Please, a little water. I'm thirsty.' She opened a bottle of milk, gave him a drink, and then covered him up again. He then said, 'Stand at the tent flap. If anyone comes by and asks you, 'Is there anyone here?' tell him, 'No, not a soul.' Then while he was fast asleep with exhaustion . . ." (Judges 4:17-21 The Message)

It's an incredible scene to imagine: Sisera, the proud Canaanite military leader, left behind his stuck chariots and his slaughtered army as he fled *for his life*. Fully aware of the dire consequences, he was determined not to be captured. This kind of fear was completely new to him and caused him to run even faster to reach a place where he believed a friend could help. He heads to Heber the

Kenite's home. (Remember Heber? The one "riding the fence"?) There, Sisera hopes to find safety and security to survive another day.

It was Jael who stepped out of her tent to meet him. You get the sense that she'd been waiting. She probably knew about the battle and may have even seen signs of war in the distance. She understood the cruelty of King Jabin and Sisera toward God's people, her people. With her husband away, this was her home—the tent belonged to her. So, when she saw Sisera stumbling into the clearing, she went out to meet him to extend the proper hospitality to her husband's friend.

She led him into the coolness of the tent, away from the scorching sun. He was like a wild animal fleeing, exhausted, scared, and seeking shelter. She then covered him with a blanket and when he asked for water, she offered him thick, rich milk instead. The milk worked its magic, and heavy in his stomach, it helped him fall into a much-needed sleep.

" . . . Jael wife of Heber took a tent peg and hammer, tiptoed toward him, and drove the tent peg through his temple and all the way to the ground. He convulsed and died." (Judges 4:21 Message)

Maybe the snores of Sisera began to fill Jael's tent, or perhaps it was the relaxed, heavy breathing of sleep that she heard, which signaled her to act. Whatever it was, at just the right moment, she sprang into action. She understood how serious this moment was and, without hesitation, reached for the tools of her trade—she was a tent-dwelling woman, and she was the one responsible for putting up the tents, not the men. In one hand, she held a sharp, iron tent peg; in the other, a heavy mallet.

Quietly, she moved through the tent to reach the spot where Sisera felt safe. Jael swung the heavy mallet and, with a decisive blow, drove the tent peg through Sisera's temple, pinning him to the ground. His sense of safety in a friend's tent ultimately led to his death. Although her husband, Heber, was unsure which side to support, Jael made her choice. She didn't stay neutral; she had chosen her side. It wasn't with the enemies of God and His people.

And Sisera **"convulsed and died." (Judges 4:21 The Message)** Later, when Barak arrived, Jael led him inside the tent to see the lifeless Sisera, not killed by a soldier with weapons of war, but rather by the tools of a tent dweller used by her own hand—a woman's hand—just as Deborah had foretold.

A FEW MORE THOUGHTS

Usually, the end of the story also marks the end of the chapter. However, this time, I want to discuss a little more. We've covered so much—history, characters, action, intrigue, unexpected twists—that we might overlook the beauty of Jael's story. I don't want that to happen. I'd like to share some simple thoughts with you.

It seems Jael understood everything—or at least most of it—that Barak didn't. While he was driven by fear, she wasn't afraid. She wasn't ashamed of who she was or where she came from. Even when her husband (good ol' Heber) made the wrong choice, she stood up for what was right. She knew that God was working before, around, through, and even after her. Because of this,

she engaged the enemy,

subdued the enemy,

and ultimately eradicated him.

And the way she did this was by simply using what she had, doing what she could, when she could. Because of that, Jael was exalted.

Maybe that's the secret to nailing it in our walk with God:

- Never let fear dominate you. Instead, surrender to the One who has no fear— the Holy Spirit—and let Him give you strength when you feel weak.

Understand that God always goes ahead of you, desires to work through you, is always present, and always has your back. Determine to use whatever you have in order to do what you can for Him.

GOING DEEPER

- Have you ever underestimated what God could do through you or someone else? Describe that experience and share the outcome.
- Can you recall a time in your life when you chose to follow your own way instead of His? How did that make you feel? How did it impact you and those around you? Are there things we can do to guide ourselves toward His way instead of our own?
- Like the last question, have you ever let fear prevent you from doing what you knew God wanted you to do? What triggered the fear and doubt? Are you willing to share this with the group and talk about how we can trust God more personally? Together?
- Do you have any thoughts about Jael and her story that weren't covered in the chapter? Would you like to discuss them with the group?

Never underestimate the power of an ordinary woman willing to be used of God.

When God's people choose to do things their own way instead of His, it always leads to oppression and trouble.

Nothing in God's Word is accidental.

ONE-HIT WONDER: RALPH ELLISON

It took Ralph Ellison seven years to write *Invisible Man* (not to be confused with *The Invisible Man* by HG Wells). This is the only book Ellison ever had published. He was a one-hit book wonder.

CHAPTER NINE

(Exodus 1)

They Put Their Careers on the Line

With the threat of losing their careers—
and much more—Shiphrah and Puah
boldly defied their ruler's edict.

There are many characters we've become familiar with through Sunday School, children's church, vacation Bible school, and sermons. However, a few we haven't met—or perhaps we've only skimmed over. Let's explore two leading ladies in the divine drama of God's people who truly deserve our attention.

Long before Shadrach, Meshach and Abednego refused to bow before Nero . . .

Before Daniel slept with lions in the den . . .

Many years before Peter and John stood tall before the religious rulers of their day . . .

or Paul was imprisoned for following Jesus . . .

there were Shiphrah and Puah.

Although their names may seem unimpressive and forgettable, they are not merely extras in the story. They have a significant role as they engage in a high-stakes power struggle with the King of Egypt, which will pave the way for the eventual and ultimate defiance of the Israelites that will lead to their freedom. Now, their names are recorded for generations to come! But before we meet these two women, let's go back in time and delve into the story of Joseph.

A Little Background: The Beginning

"These are the names of the Israelites who came to Egypt with Jacob along with their households: Reuben, Simeon, Levi, and Judah, Issachar, Zebulun, and Benjamin, Dan and Naphtali, Gad and Asher.
"The total number in Jacob's family was seventy. Joseph was already in Egypt.
"Eventually, Joseph, his brothers, and everyone in his generation died. But the Israelites were fertile and became populous. They multiplied and grew dramatically, filling the whole land."
(Exodus 1:1-7 CEB)

It all began with the dreamer. You remember Joseph—the youngest of Jacob's eleven sons. He was his father's favorite, doted on and given dreams by *the* Father. An irritation to his brothers, his story takes many twists and turns:

thrown in the pit,
sold to the Ishmaelites,
slave in the palace,
thrown into prison,
and finally . . .

Pharaoh's right-hand man (according to Andrew Lloyd Weber).

Years pass.

Famine hits.

Joseph's brothers are hungry.

So, they go to Egypt seeking grain.

They have to go before their brother Joseph.

They don't know it's him—He knows them.

They grovel and grovel some more.

Joseph forgives.

Reunited in Egypt.

This marks the beginning of our story and provides context for verses 1-7. It describes how the Israelites arrived in Egypt. They weren't forced by whips and chains, nor were they dragged in shackles. It was through God's favor shown to His people via His chosen man. (For more details, start reading in Genesis 37. Go ahead and dive in; you won't want to put the Book down!)

THE ENDING

**"After the child had grown up,
she brought him back to Pharaoh's
daughter, who adopted him as her son.
She named him Moses, 'because,' she said,
'I pulled him out of the water.'"
(Exodus 2:10 CEB)**

To fully appreciate the significance of these two ladies, we have to leap forward centuries to the story of Moses. God is always at work. His presence may go unnoticed—perhaps even questioned at times—but He is working all things together for the good of His people. Do you remember the story?

Pharoah commands, "Drown the boy babies!"

Moses' mom and dad placed him in a basket.

They put the basket in the tall grass along the Nile River.

Pharaoh's daughter is bathing in this very river.

Moses starts to cry, and she saves the boy.

He was raised in Pharaoh's court as a prince.

He has received the best of everything.

God has greater plans for Moses than they knew.

He would deliver God's people from Egypt.

That's the culmination of our story. If you'd like to revisit this story, start reading in Exodus 2.

Without the story *between these stories,* the Israelites might never have been born into a new life of freedom. Birthed—that's a great description. This story is the story of two midwives.

THE MIDDLE OF THE STORY

Paul Harvey was a well-known commentator for ABC News Radio from 1951 to 2008. On May 10, 1976, he debuted a new program titled "The Rest of the Story." Listeners enjoyed hearing the backstories behind famous events and figures. This quickly became one of his most beloved lines: "And now, for the rest of the story." If he were narrating the story of the redemption, exodus, and deliverance of God's people from Egypt's bondage, *this* would be the rest of the story...

Nearly 400 years pass between Exodus 1:7 and 8. During that time, we read that a new Pharaoh came to reign over Egypt. Remember, Egypt was the only "superpower" during this period, which would make the Pharaoh the most powerful man in the world. He was not only a ruler but also considered a deity—a son of the gods.

Throughout those four centuries, the Israelites—God's chosen people—were blessed and continued to thrive. Due to their rapid growth, Pharaoh felt threatened by their numbers, prompting him to enslave them.

This resulted in years of servitude during which they were treated like inferior people. The Egyptians despised them. Pharaoh and his people had forgotten Joseph and the contributions he made to their nation. Consequently, the favor shown to Joseph and his descendants was reversed and erased. They found themselves in their first exile. Everything seemed turned upside down for God's chosen people.

Pharaoh's plan was to break them. It seems his desire was to work them to death: Make them so busy that it would slow their growth and eventually destroy them. And really, this begins a downward spiral of evil displayed by the King of Egypt. The destruction of the Israelites would be his ultimate goal.

Have you noticed that evil unchecked always tends to get worse and worse? It leads to compromise upon compromise. It begins the death spin of society and is actually the nature of sin. Evil will always eliminate life. Think about it. All throughout history, this is the pattern:

- Pharaoh (tried to drown Hebrew male infants so the Hebrew women would eventually marry Egyptian men and eventually terminating the Jewish race)
- King Herod (killed babies in an effort to kill Jesus)
- Adolf Hitler (orchestrated the genocide of 6 million Jews and the deaths of tens of millions more through a campaign of racial purity)

- Mao Zedong (orchestrated the Great Leap Forward and Cultural Revolution leading to tens of millions of deaths)
- Joseph Stalin (Established a totalitarian regime leading to the deaths of millions)
- Pol Pot (orchestrated the killing of 1.5 to 2 million in the Cambodian Genocide)

Evil always looks to destroy and eliminate life.

This was the goal: Destroy and crush God's people.

But Pharaoh's plan failed.

Instead of working them to death, they flourished and continued to grow. So Pharoah devised another plan.

GOD'S HEROINES

If you read through the list of Jacob's sons in 1:1-7 and the naming of Moses in 2:10, you'll find only two names mentioned. There are many characters (Pharaoh, a man from the tribe of Levi, the baby's sister, and others), but only two individuals whose names appear: Shiphrah and Puah.

This.

Is.

A.

Big.

Deal.

Because they're named, we're able to see their significance. Names matter and theirs is recorded. Just to highlight this, notice Pharaoh. It's already been acknowledged that he was considered to be the most important, powerful man in the world in his day. Pharaoh was considered to be deity—a god—since he was the son of gods. Yet, in the book of Exodus his title (pharaoh) is used 107 times, but his name is never mentioned. Sure, we can look back in history and determine who would have been pharaoh during this time period, but it's not recorded in God's historical record, His book.

And that matters.

To be named was a big deal.

To have your name blotted out was terrible:

> **"You have rebuked the nations,**
> **you have destroyed the wicked;**
> **you have blotted out their**
> **name forever and ever."**
> **(Psalm 9:5 NKJV)**

In the midst of all the anonymity of Exodus 1:7-2:10, they're named:

Shiphrah and Puah. They're recorded so that all generations can remember them and their remarkable story.

WHAT'S THE STORY?

They were midwives. In Egyptian culture, midwifery was a respected profession. Their role was to assist in childbirth, providing care for both the mother and child throughout the entire birthing process. This was an esteemed position. The midwives held the privilege of announcing the newborn's sex, being the first to see the baby and reporting to an anxiously waiting mother: "It's a boy!" or "It's a girl!"

Being a midwife carried tremendous responsibility. It was certainly a special position. Yet, they served the enslaved Israelites. Most believe Shiphrah and Puah were Egyptians—not Hebrews. If that's the case, they were in a subservient role to a subservient people.

It's believed that these two weren't just midwives, but *head midwives.* They would oversee all the other midwives who assisted the Hebrew women during childbirth. That was likely why Pharaoh spoke directly to them about his plan:

"The king of Egypt spoke to two Hebrew midwives named Shiphrah and Puah: " 'When you are helping the Hebrew women give birth and you see the baby being born, if it's a boy, kill him. But if it's a girl, you can let her live.' " (Exodus 1:15-16 CEB)

Again, you can see that evil always seeks to destroy life. When Pharaoh was unable to break the children of Israel by working them to death, he took the next step. He ordered them killed at birth. When new life was just beginning, he snuffed it out. They would never have a chance. With the male children being eliminated, the

Hebrew race would eventually be extinguished, and the threat of uprising would go with them.

The plan hinged on the leadership and obedience of these two women. If they did not follow instructions, an entire race would be erased. What would they do?

We can't overlook the dilemma in which Shiphrah and Puah were placed. The most powerful man in the world—Pharoah—gave them their orders.

The.

Most.

Powerful.

Man.

In.

The.

World.

Had given them a direct command.

Remember, he was seen as a deity by the Egyptians. This order from the king was meant to be obeyed. You followed what Pharaoh said, or else. He literally held their lives in his hands. And he commanded the midwives: "Kill the newborn male children!"

But Shiphrah and Puah feared God:

"The midwives, however, feared God and did not do what the king of Egypt had told them to do; they let the boys live." (Exodus 1:17 HCSB)

They feared God, so they disregarded the wicked command of an Egyptian god. They had a profound reverence for the *Hebrew* God, which moved them beyond the concern of facing punishment from a man who was merely deemed a deity. Something about this God inspired an overwhelming respect not only for who He was but also for an understanding of who His people were. Therefore, they allowed the boys to live.

Let's pause for a moment to consider what they did. They took an enormous risk because they were more concerned about pleasing God than man. What a tremendous lesson for us to learn: We must always choose the fear of God over the fear of man. That choice will be revealed in our everyday lives.

- When we choose to fear man, we will always promote ourselves.
- When we live in the fear of God, we will always promote Him.
- When we live to please people, it will lead to compromise.
- When we live to please God, we stand on His principles, His promises.
- Fearing man will always promote the need to self-protect.
- Fearing God causes us to be willing to risk all for His glory.

Even if they were not Hebrews, Shiphrah and Puah had come to know God. This knowledge prompted them to defy a direct order from Pharaoh. They chose to do what was right in God's eyes. They allowed the boys to live!

By sparing the lives of these newborn male babies, they become champions for life. We've already stated that evil always seeks to destroy life, and we've witnessed this in Pharaoh's command. Naturally, the opposite is true of good. Good protects and honors life. Why? Because that's what God does. He cares for the "least of these." That's precisely what they accomplished. By sparing the lives of the helpless, they honored the God who created them in His image.

This is another great place for us to stop and reflect: Real heroes honor life as God does. While grieving the loss of so many children who never had a chance at life due to abortion, we must remember that *all* life matters to Him. It's easy to value people who are incredibly talented, attractive, smart, or entertaining...

But what about those whom the world doesn't value? Or the person who has nothing to give in return? The outcast. The handicapped. The addict. Here's how Proverbs 31 guides us:

"Speak up for those who cannot speak for themselves, for the rights of all who are destitute. Speak up and judge fairly; defend the rights of the poor and needy." (Proverbs 31:8-9 NIV)

God values all lives. As His people, we should, too. In his beloved children's book *Horton Hears a Who*, Dr. Suess says, "A person's a person, no matter how small."

Shiphrah and Puah honored God by honoring life. They defied Pharaoh's command by sparing the lives of the newborn Hebrew boys. Midwives held a subservient position within a subservient people, and yet in God's eyes, they are champions!

HEY! WHERE ARE ALL THESE BABY BOYS COMING FROM?

"The king of Egypt called in the midwives. 'Why didn't you obey my orders? You've let those babies live!' " (Exodus 1:18 The Message)

You can imagine that eventually, the secret will come out. Pharaoh will notice that there are baby boys around. Then, there's going to be trouble.

Shiphrah and Puah were summoned once again before Pharaoh. Imagine how they might have felt. They heard every step as they made their way down the corridor to Pharaoh's throne room. They anxiously awaited his words while butterflies fluttered in their stomachs. As he gazed in their direction, the silence was shattered by a loud, "WHY?! You've allowed those babies to live!"

Here's Shiphrah and Puah's response:

"The midwives answered Pharaoh, 'Hebrew women are not like Egyptian women; they are vigorous and give birth before the midwives arrive.'"
(Exodus 2:19 NIV)

Amazingly, Pharaoh seemed satisfied with their response. Or at least there wouldn't be any gallows for them. He spared their lives. Actually,

"God was pleased with the midwives. The people continued to increase in number—a very strong people. "And because the midwives honored God, God gave them families of their own."
(Exodus 1:20-21 The Message)

God was pleased. What a beautiful phrase. Listen to it again: God was pleased. Because He was pleased, He gave them families of their own. Because they honored God, God honored them. This reminds us that doing the right thing matters—no matter what the cost. Obedience makes a difference, and God always honors obedience with His blessing.

Do you want God to be pleased with you? There's no greater desire in my heart than to live a life pleasing to Him. When we reflect on this story, we cannot ignore the principle that God rewards faithfulness.

You never go wrong by doing what's right.

It matters.

The temptation is to choose the easy path or to settle for half measures in our obedience. However, partial obedience isn't true obedience.

If we want to live lives that are pleasing to Him, obedience is required.

Complete obedience.

Unconditional obedience.

That's the obedience that God rewards.

Blessings follow obedience!

Shiphrah and Puah feared God, and He was pleased with them.

He was kind to them. He blessed their obedience.

HIS STORY

We all have a role to play in God's story. This message shouts from the obscure story we find situated between the stories of Joseph and Moses. It resides in the heart of God's redemptive story of His people. Shiphrah and Puah—two midwives—played a significant role in the deliverance of God's people.

Now, Pharaoh devises another scheme: all male children up to a certain age will drown in the Nile. Thus begins the story of Moses and the Exodus. But without Shiphrah and Puah, it may never have been.

God's redemptive story is still being written today, and you have a part to fulfill which may seem insignificant to you, but no one is unimportant in His drama. As we embrace our supporting roles, may we always remember the lessons learned from Shiphrah and Puah:

- Choose to fear God rather than man.
- Honor all life just as God honors all life.
- You never go wrong by doing what's right.
- God honors obedience with blessing.

GOING DEEPER:

- **What is an area of your life where you need to fear God rather than man?**
- **Do you need to examine or rethink your views on the ways in which you value life? Is there someone that you can express the love of God to this week?**
- **Are you living a faithful life? Are you completely obedient to Him, walking in all the light that you've been given?**

Real heroes honor life like God does.

We all have a part to play in God's story.

We must always choose the fear of God over the fear of man.

Doing the right thing matters—no matter what the cost. Obedience makes a difference.

ONE-HIT WONDER:

AARON KRAUSE and SPONGE DADDY

It's the sponge with a smiley face. Aaron Krause was a car detailer working to develop a polishing pad that was sold to 3M in 2008. He also created a sponge that becomes soft in warm water and hard in cold water, but he put it on a shelf and forgot about it.

That is, *until.*

Five years later, Aaron was cleaning some lawn furniture and remembered the sponges he had made. He then tested the sponges on dirty dishes and got the same great result.

Aaron took his sponges to TVs "Shark Tank," where Lori Greiner partnered with him to go public. The next day, they sold 42,000 sponges in just over five minutes. And the rest is history . . . with another one-hit wonder.

CHAPTER TEN

Part One

(1 Kings 22:1-40)

He Knew the Voice of God

We navigate countless voices every day. Discerning which ones are worth listening to takes wisdom. Micaiah was determined to follow God's voice when a multitude of others were screaming in his face.

"For three years there was no war between Aram and Israel. Then during the third year, King Jehoshaphat of Judah went to visit King Ahab of Israel. During the visit, the king of Israel said to his officials, 'Do you realize that the town of Ramoth-gilead belongs to us? And yet we've done nothing to recapture it from the king of Aram!' Then he turned to Jehoshaphat and asked, 'Will you join me in battle to recover Ramoth-gilead?'

"Jehoshaphat replied to the king of Israel, 'Why, of course! You and I are as one.

My troops are your troops, and my horses are your horses.' Then Jehoshaphat added, 'But first let's find out what the LORD says.'

"So the king of Israel summoned the prophets, about four hundred of them, and asked them, 'Should I go to war against Ramoth-gilead, or should I hold back?'

"They all replied, 'Yes, go right ahead! The Lord will give the king victory.'

"But Jehoshaphat asked, 'Is there not also a prophet of the LORD here? We should ask him the same question.'

"The king of Israel replied to Jehoshaphat, 'There is one more man who could consult the LORD for us, but I hate him. He never prophesies anything but trouble for me! His name is Micaiah son of Imlah.'

"Jehoshaphat replied, 'That's not the way a king should talk! Let's hear what he has to say.'

"So the king of Israel called one of his officials and said, 'Quick! Bring Micaiah son of Imlah.'" (1 Kings 22:1-9 NLT)

IS THERE A PROPHET OF THE LORD?

Israel was divided. The once-unified people, under both King David and Solomon, now lived in two kingdoms, two realities, with two separate futures.

King Ahab ruled the northern kingdom from a golden throne, but his heart was as hard as stone. His marriage to Jezebel did more than create political alliances; it brought the gods of Tyre, the altars of Baal, and many false prophets eager to flatter Ahab with whatever he wanted to hear. Any man who dared speak the truth to the king faced danger.

Because of this, God's prophets didn't get the red-carpet treatment at court—they weren't welcomed at all. Anyone who dared oppose the king paid a steep price. Still, there were always those who wouldn't—perhaps, couldn't—stay silent. Micaiah was one of them.

Micaiah [mick-KYE-yah] means "who is like Yahweh?" or "who is like God?" His name quietly challenged a kingdom where the One True God had been replaced by inanimate statues; a place where creation was worshiped instead of the Creator. No one knows Micaiah's origins or how he was called to be a prophet. Unlike Elijah, he didn't become famous for making grand gestures or performing miracles.

When he spoke, however, his words carried enough truth to strike King Ahab like a chisel against stone. Because of this, Ahab avoided him, preferring prophets who assured him of victories, blessings, and a hopeful future. Micaiah wasn't that kind of prophet, and the truth has a way of reaching those who try to ignore it.

SOMETHING'S STIRRING

Although peace had lasted for three years, conflict was on the horizon. King Ahab was secretly planning something that would soon disrupt the peace. This becomes clear during a visit from King Jehoshaphat of Judah, the southern kingdom. Ahab mentions a town on the border between their kingdoms called Ramoth-Gilead, saying, "That used to be ours. Let's take it back!"

The problem? It was controlled by the Arameans, who needed to be defeated in battle to reclaim it. Ahab's proposal to Jehoshaphat was to join him in fighting the Arameans. Ultimately, he was asking Jehoshaphat to participate in a military campaign against these nomads from the Syrian desert fringe. The Arameans were tough opponents; they were warrior peoples, and Ahab wanted to go to war against them. After some discussion, Jehoshaphat agreed with one condition,

". . . let's find out what the LORD says."
(1 Kings 22:5 NLT).

This is a good time to pause and reflect. Interestingly, Jehoshaphat mainly focused on listening to God's guidance, while Ahab pursued his own path. Above all, that was the king of Judah's priority. He understood they could only succeed if God approved their actions. It makes me wonder if we approach life the same way. I know I (Billy) can be impulsive at times, acting on emotion and doing what I want without first praying about it. When I mention this, I'm not talking about serious or sinful issues, but rather everyday matters.

JEHOSHAPHAT = GOOD GUY

Historically, Jehoshaphat was seen as a good king because of his devotion to God. During his leadership, Judah experienced many religious reforms, along with times of peace and prosperity. Don't get me wrong, he wasn't perfect—he made mistakes and sometimes rushed ahead without waiting on God—but he was learning to put Jehovah first, and overall, he was a good king.

I guess I'm saying I want to improve. I want to work toward becoming someone who cares more about what God says than about my own desires. What about you? Will you join me in that? Okay, let's get back to the story.

"So the king of Israel brought together the prophets—about four hundred men—and asked them, 'Shall I go to war against Ramoth-Gilead, or shall I refrain?'

" 'Go,' they answered, 'for the Lord will give it into the king's hand.' "
(1 Kings 22:6 NIV)

The court prophets were called one by one, all giving a similar response to Ahab:

"Go!"

"It's a fantastic plan, king!"

"Do it!"

"You've got this, king!"

"Victory is certain!"

"Arameans—go start the bus!"

"You da' man!"

Do you see the picture? All four hundred of the so-called prophets in the king's court agreed it was a great idea, even though it was a disastrous one. The room buzzed with excited voices, exaggerated promises, and predictions that seemed carefully orchestrated, but King Jehoshaphat remained unimpressed.

"But Jehoshaphat dragged his heels: 'Is there still another prophet of GOD we can consult?' "
(1 Kings 22:7 The Message)

As the tension in the room grew thicker, Jehoshaphat felt a shiver run down his spine. Something was wrong. The four hundred prophets weren't seeking guidance from his God but were consulting Baal and Asherah's gods (see 1 Kings 16:29-33), influenced by his wife Jezebel. Now, Jehoshaphat wants to hear from his God again, so he asks once more.

UH-OH

Ahab's expression shifted from excitement to dread as a particular name entered his mind—a name he wanted to avoid because of this prophet's persistent nagging in the past. The name felt too familiar, so he was uninterested in hearing what the prophet had to say. Still, Jehoshaphat's question required him to respond.

It's easy to imagine a prominent figure—whether a politician, sports star, actor, or pastor—surrounded by yes men who always agree. These people boost their ego and affirm that everything they say or want is correct. King Ahab was one such person. He pretended to care about God's words but ultimately sought his own way. He was scheming, manipulative, and used religious language to push his own agenda. He was not the first, nor the last, to do so. But King Jehoshaphat saw through his schemes and remained skeptical. He had forced Ahab's hand; he sighed and with annoyance in his voice, responded with a name he was reluctant to speak.

" 'There is one more man who could consult the Lord for us, but I hate him. He never prophesies anything but trouble for me! His name is Micaiah son of Imlah.' "
(1 Kings 22:8 NLT)

If Ahab's reluctance to call Micaiah didn't already reveal his feelings about the prophet, his words now make it unmistakably clear. The king resented Micaiah because his stubborn heart preferred comforting lies over difficult truths. Ahab liked flattery from deceitful prophets more than honest advice that might challenge his plans.

The four hundred prophets were mostly hired to give favorable "prophecies" that supported Ahab's ambitions. Micaiah, on the other hand, delivered a genuine message from God. Because of this, Ahab hated Micaiah and didn't want to listen to him.

SEEM FAMILIAR?

We all recognize that feeling, don't we? We've all experienced it. If the advice we get doesn't match our hopes or wishes, what do we do? We seek a second opinion. If Mom's advice doesn't seem right, we turn to Dad. I'll say it again—we've all been there. But tuning in the voices that agree with us and avoiding the ones that challenge us ~~is~~ a big mistake. In fact, it can lead to all kinds of problems: spiritual stagnation, compromised morals, and even hardened hearts. What's more, it compromises Christian accountability, which we all need to grow in our relationship with Christ.

Without those other voices, an environment develops where sin goes unchallenged and self-absorption and ego protection take priority over the truth. This creates a false sense of security, similar to what was cultivated in King Ahab's court. That was the situation he found himself in, and Jehoshaphat was not impressed.

King Jehoshaphat raised his eyebrows, uneasy with Ahab's reaction. He noticed that the Israeli king had surrounded himself with sycophants and false prophets, showing poor judgment. He sat upright and said,

" 'That's not the way a king should talk!
Let's hear what he has to say.' "
(1 Kings 22:8 NLT)

If Ahab wanted Judah's support in the war, he had little choice. He clearly disliked the prophet Micaiah but hesitated to upset Jehoshaphat. Reluctantly, he rolled his eyes and let out a heavy sigh before calling for a messenger:

"So the king of Israel called one of his officials and said, "Quick! Bring Micaiah son of Imlah." (1 Kings 22:9 NLT)

WHAT A CIRCUS!

"King Ahab of Israel and King Jehoshaphat of Judah, dressed in their royal robes, were sitting on thrones at the threshing floor near the gate of Samaria. All of Ahab's prophets were prophesying there in front of them. One of them, Zedekiah son of Kenaanah, made some iron horns and proclaimed, 'This is what the Lord says: With these horns you will gore the Arameans to death!'

"All the other prophets agreed. 'Yes,' they said, 'go up to Ramoth-gilead and be victorious, for the Lord will give the king victory!' " (1 Kings 22:10-12 NLT)

What an incredible scene! The king of Israel and the king of Judah sat on their thrones, dressed in royal robes, at the threshing floor near the Gate of Samaria. In front of them, all four hundred of Ahab's prophets were prophesying.

It was a spectacle, and the message was that God would destroy the Arameans—they would be gored to death! It was like a pep rally before a big game, with confetti in the air, the band playing, and cheerleaders leading chants, promising certain victory.

This was a political-military rally full of bravado and hubris. But here's the point: It didn't matter what public opinion said or what seemed inevitable from a human perspective. Only what God said truly mattered, and they were about to learn that. Remember, a messenger was sent to get Micaiah, who would ultimately thunder amid all the hysteria, "Thus says the Lord!"

Micaiah was removed from the theatrics of the king of Israel's court. He had long since worn out his welcome there. His dwelling was somewhere far from the luxury of the palace, in a simple, discreet place. Much like his life. Surely, he had heard about the events taking place. He was aware of the hysteria—the bands, the crowd's cheers, the prophecy of the fake prophets—everyone was of one mind, except for him.

He was happily alone when a knock sounded at his door. Ahab's messenger hurriedly made his way through the streets of Samaria, weaving through narrow alleyways and dodging movement to reach Micaiah's house.

When the door opened, the messenger saw the prophet. However, Micaiah wasn't dressed like the other court prophets, and he was known (as we've already seen) for not living in King Ahab's shadow. His loyalty seemed to be to another King. With this knowledge, the messenger approached cautiously and spoke as if advising a fool before risking his own head. This is what he said:

"Meanwhile, the messenger who went to get Micaiah said to him, "Look, all the prophets are promising victory for the king. Be sure that you agree with them and promise success." (1 Kings 22:13 NLT)

Sadly, it's easy to understand his message. He was saying that all the other prophets were saying the same thing, so all he needed to do was be reasonable.

Follow the rules.

Say something positive like them.

Don't rock the boat.

They've promised the king victory, so now you do the same. With a smile on his face—not a smile of agreement, but one from someone who seemed to have heard this advice before—he responded without hesitation:

"As surely as the Lord lives, I will say only what the Lord tells me to say." (1 Kings 22:14 NLT)

The journey back to the palace was probably quiet because the messenger sensed that things wouldn't turn out well. Micaiah never knew how to dance to the music, nor was he skilled or inclined to craft his words to win over the powerful. Instead, he simply told the truth, boldly and without fear, even when it wasn't welcomed. The messenger carried a sense of dread and a knot in his stomach, aware of what was coming.

The prophet walked with the calm of someone who owed nothing to anyone, confident that truth was on his side. It's incredible when you think about the immense pressure he faced. After all, he was an Israelite too.

These were his people.

This was his country.

He wanted to be a good citizen.

There was political, national, and religious pressure for him to be a good Israelite. And, of course, there was the personal pressure of wanting to avoid persecution or punishment for speaking the truth. Still, he walked in peace. Why? Remember his promise: "I will say only what the Lord tells me."

Those are words to live by. What the Lord says, that's what we speak. That's what we stick to. We won't get ahead of what He says, nor will we ignore it. I've tried to be mindful of this in my ministry.

As an evangelist and preacher of the Gospel, there's a real danger of preaching what I want to say rather than what He wants me to. Honestly, that's a very real temptation. However, I know I will give an account of everything I've preached to every congregation. And on that day, I want to be able to say, "What the Lord says, that's what I spoke."

WE'RE ALL RESPONSIBLE

The same principle applies to everyone. Sure, not all of us are evangelists, pastors, or preachers, but we're all witnesses. Acts 1:8 reminds us that witnessing isn't just something we do; it's who we are. That's the promise of that verse. Our entire lives should point to Him, and the only way that happens is when we decide that whatever He says, that's what we'll speak.

That's how we'll live. Did Micaiah choose to live this way? So far in the story, we've seen that he wasn't there to give opinions. He wasn't even there to share hopes, wishes, or dreams. Certainly, he wasn't there to offer hot takes to attract attention to himself. We hope he was there to speak what the Lord said, to draw attention to Him and Him alone. Will you live your life the same way?

Let's pause the story here and pick it up in the next chapter and discover what Micaiah will do. Meanwhile, here are a few things to consider.

GOING DEEPER

- **Identify a time you felt pressured to go along with the crowd. What was the outcome?**
- **Have you ever taken a bold stand for God when those around you were doing the opposite? If so, describe the situation.**
- **Can you recall a time when you were ostracized for doing what was right?**

MICAIAH IS . . .

a. living in the king's palace.
b. running for political office.
c. an Old Testament prophet.
d. the cover story for the "Ramoth-Gilead Times."

KING AHAB IS . . .

a. searching for a new political cabinet.
b. married to Queen Jezebel.
c. ruler of Egypt.
d. a godly king.

KING AHAB'S FOUR HUNDRED PROPHETS ARE . . .

a. singing the "Hallelujah Chorus."
b. quoting Scripture.
c. full of deceit.
d. running for office.

God's prophets didn't get the red-carpet treatment at court.

As the tension in the room grew thicker, Jehoshaphat felt a shiver run down his spine.

He was aware of the hysteria.

CHAPTER ELEVEN

Part Two

(1 Kings 22:1-40)

He Knew the Voice of God

Let's continue Micaiah's story as he navigates a high-stakes situation in King Ahab's court, deciding whether to agree with four hundred prophets or to speak God's truth.

When Micaiah arrived in King Ahab's court before "his wickedness" and good King Jehoshaphat, he could've shouted, "You can't handle the truth, Ahab!"

And he would've been right. But let's check out what actually happened.

"When Micaiah arrived before the king, Ahab asked him, 'Micaiah, should we go to war against Ramoth-gilead, or should we hold back?'

"Micaiah replied sarcastically, 'Yes, go up and be victorious, for the Lord will give the king victory!'

"But the king replied sharply, 'How many times must I demand that you speak only the truth to me when you speak for the Lord?' "
(1 Kings 22:15-16 NLT)

When they arrived, the hall was packed and still filled with the hysteria of false prophets eagerly staging visions of victory. One of them, Zedekiah, was waving a set of iron horns in the air, shouting about destroying the enemy and goring them to death. All of this made King Ahab smile with satisfaction until he saw Micaiah enter the room, at which point his smile turned into a scowl, and suddenly the mood of the entire room shifted.

As Micaiah approached the throne, all eyes were on him, and he knew it. The atmosphere was thick with anticipation and suspicion, almost tangible. Yet, he moved with steady confidence, walking deliberately and studying the room as if he understood the situation completely. King Ahab, misled by the false prophets' lies into a false sense of security, now appeared tense. Something about Micaiah deeply unsettled him.

Sitting upright on his throne, he prepared for the confrontation and asked, "Should we go to war or not?" The king crossed his arms, forced a smile, and waited for the response. Micaiah was never one to sugarcoat things or give the king an answer just to please him.

And now, standing before him, he was ready to do what he always did: speak the truth, whether the king wanted to hear it or not. Ahab, however, wasn't prepared for his response. With a tilted head and a tone bordering on mockery, Micaiah replied, **"Yes, go to war and be victorious, for the Lord will give the king victory!"**

What?!?

Silence fell in the room after his words. This wasn't the answer they expected. Nor was it what King Ahab anticipated. Something was off with this reply—it echoed the message of the other prophets but lacked their enthusiasm. In fact, it sounded insincere.

Recognizing this, Ahab leaned forward with a frown, realizing there was more to this prophet's message. His frustration was revealed as he shouted,

"How many times must I demand that you speak only the truth to me when you speak for the Lord?" (1 Kings 22:16 NLT)

Micaiah's demeanor changed as he began to respond to King Ahab's demand. With his head held high and a serious tone, he delivered this message:

"In a vision I saw all Israel scattered on the mountains, like sheep without a shepherd. And the Lord said, 'Their master has been killed. Send them home in peace.'" (Judges 22:17 NLT)

THE REAL NEWS

His voice sliced through the air like a sharp blade and pierced the king's heart. The silence became deafening, as it didn't take a very wise man to understand what was being said. Micaiah had just prophesied that Ahab would not return home from battle; he would be killed. He demanded the truth, but he couldn't handle the truth.

The king's expression briefly paled at Micaiah's prophecy, but he quickly regained his composure. His face soon flushed red with anger as he straightened up, snorted, and shot a look at King Jehoshaphat. With a tone of sarcasm and irritation, he declared,

" 'See! What did I tell you? He never has a good word for me from God, only doom.' " (1 Kings 22:18 Message)

It was a clear 'I told you so' moment, and the hall seemed to murmur in agreement, but the prophet hadn't finished. Micaiah's gaze remained steady and piercing, as if he could see something the others could not. The silence that settled over everyone was thick and heavy, and no one dared to interrupt.

Motionless and with a backbone of steel, the prophet's gaze was fixed on Ahab as if he were seeing far beyond that room of flattery and deceit. The king tried to disguise his annoyance with a half-smile as his hand gripped the arm of his throne tightly, as Micaiah's voice echoed firmly:

Micaiah kept on: "I'm not done yet; listen to God's word:

I saw God enthroned,
and all the angel armies of heaven
Standing at attention
ranged on his right and his left.
And God said, 'How can we seduce Ahab
into attacking Ramoth Gilead?'
Some said this,
and some said that.
Then a bold angel stepped out,
stood before God, and said,
'I'll seduce him.'
'And how will you do it?' said God.
'Easy,' said the angel,
'I'll get all the prophets to lie.'
'That should do it,' said God.
'On your way—seduce him!'

"And that's what has happened. God filled the mouths of your puppet prophets with seductive lies. God has pronounced your doom."

(1 Kings 22:19-23 The Message)

As he said those words, they seemed to hang heavily in the air. Some people exchanged uneasy glances, while others grew visibly angrier. When the final accusation and claim of puppet prophets were made, Zedekiah, their leader, reached his breaking point. As his swelling pride began to crack, Zedekiah's face turned red with rage. He could no longer contain his anger toward Micaiah's insolence.

THE TRUTH ISN'T ALWAYS EASY TO ACCEPT

The Lord's message, which he delivered, rebuked both Ahab and the prophets—calling them liars—which created almost unbearable tension in the court. Zedekiah, unrestrained, stepped toward Micaiah and, with a quick gesture, slapped him across the face, the dry sound echoing through the hall. Trying to regain dignity, he mocked and said,

" 'Since when did the Spirit of God leave me and take up with you?' " (1 Kings 22:24 The Message)

Micaiah, refusing to back down, didn't look away as he responded with these words:

"You'll know soon enough; you'll know it when you're frantically and futilely looking for a place to hide." (1 Kings 22:25 The Message)

The room grew silent once more as Ahab stared at Micaiah with fierce anger. His knuckles turned white from clutching the arms of the throne, trying to restrain himself. But now, his patience had come to an end. With his voice filled with rage he ordered,

**" 'Get Micaiah out of here! Turn him over to Amon the city magistrate and to Joash the king's son with this message, 'King's orders: Lock him up in jail; keep him on bread and water until I'm back in one piece.' "
(1 Kings 22:26-27 The Message)**

The king delivered his sentence without hesitation. Micaiah would suffer for his words and actions. After the battle, upon his return, he would mock and further punish the disobedient prophet.

GOD'S TRUTH

Ahab had become so distant from God that he no longer recognized His voice. As he was being led away, Micaiah declared one last warning:

**"If you ever get back in one piece, I'm no prophet of God." He added, "When it happens, O people, remember where you heard it!"
(1 Kings 22:28 The Message)**

The king looked away, ignoring his words, but internally, he sensed that the truth had been spoken. Although he tried to dismiss the prophet's warning as the ranting of a bitter man, he could not deny the underlying truth. Deep down, beneath layers of pride and self-reliance, he perhaps knew they were more than just words—maybe just a warning. Ultimately, it would be God's final verdict.

If there's ever been an example of someone standing up for what's right—speaking truth to power—it's the story of Micaiah. It's hard not to genuinely admire his bravery and boldness. And what a perfect illustration of the noise that surrounds each of us.

In a room with the most powerful of two kingdoms and the voices of four hundred prophets shouting one thing, he was willing to stand and speak for God. We live in a world filled with conflicting voices shouting loudly about the direction they want the world to take.

The line between right and wrong has become so blurred that some believe there are no absolute truths and try to persuade others to accept that philosophy as well. Media shapes our thinking with a constant drumbeat of opinions they want us to adopt, and society is overwhelmed with groupthink. It's easy to follow the crowd, to blend in, and not rock the boat. But that's not what we're meant to do.

We admire Micaiah because he embodies qualities we aspire to have. He was a distinctive voice that courageously spoke the truth, even when it was unpopular. He was willing to stand out while others just blended into the culture and noise. It wasn't easy, and he knew it would come with a high price, but he spoke up—stood for God regardless. He was able to confront darkness because he was filled with His light. When our moment comes, may we be as bold and determined as he was.

THE FINAL SCENE

We can speed up the rest. King Ahab goes into battle—they head to Ramoth Gilead. Then we read,

> **"Just then someone, without aiming, shot an arrow randomly into the crowd and hit the king of Israel in the chink of his armor. The king told his charioteer, 'Turn back! Get me out of here—I'm wounded.'"**
> **(1 Kings 22:34 The Message)**

Did you see that? Someone shot an arrow without even aiming. In other words: *God's sovereignty.*

Nothing happens by accident, luck, or fortune. This was God's plan, God's will. God said it would happen, and it did.

He was shot by a random man who didn't aim at anything, and it hit and ultimately killed the king.

Micaiah was God's prophet, and his word was true!

AND THEN?

Sadly, we never learn what happened to Micaiah. You can read the rest of the chapter, the rest of the Bible, and see that we never hear about him again. We're never told what becomes of him. We do know he was sent to prison and was to be fed the 'bread of affliction,' as some translations say. For all we know, he remained there until he died because he stood for the truth. We just don't know.

We do know, however, where he is now. At some point, whether in a jail cell or peacefully at home in bed, his life ended, and he entered Heaven's gates. Can you imagine what that moment was like? No longer under the authority of an earthly king, he now hears the Divine King say,

" 'Well done, good and faithful servant. . . . Enter into the joy of your Lord.' "
(Matthew 25:23 NKJV)

That must have been an extraordinary day, and it's a day you and I can look forward to when we hear those same words.

GOING DEEPER

- **Slide into Micaiah's sandals for a moment. How would you have responded when King Ahab and four hundred prophets desired only one answer from you?**
- **Is there a time when God's Truth became blurred in your own life? What did you do about it?**
- **Share a time it was difficult for you to share God's Truth.**

It was a clear 'I told you so' moment.

As Micaiah approached the throne, all eyes were on him.

We admire Micaiah because he embodies qualities we aspire to have.

ONE-HIT WONDER: EDWARD CRAVEN WALKER

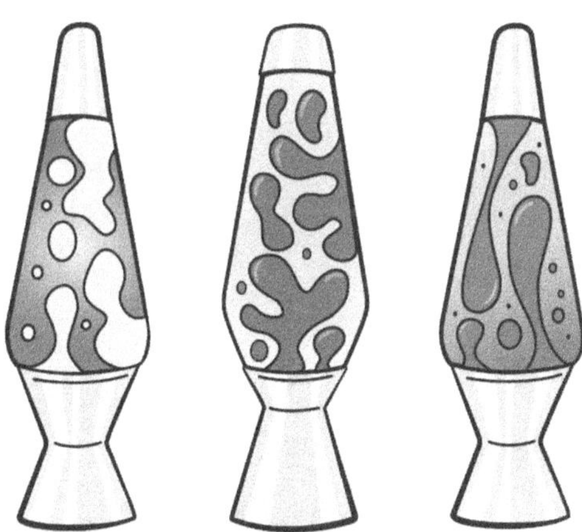

LAVA LAMP

The lava lamp was invented in 1948 by an English accountant named Edward Craven Walker. He was inspired by an egg timer made from a shaker filled with alien-looking liquids bubbling on a stovetop.

There's a lava lamp on permanent display in the Smithsonian. The world's largest lava lamp is in Soap Lake, Wash., and stands 60 ft tall! It holds 100,000 gallons of lava formula, which is a specific blend of oil and wax. The most expensive lava lamp ever sold was $15,000. And no two lava lamps are the same. What did Edward invent after the lava lamp? Nothing. He was a one-hit wonder.

CHAPTER TWELVE

(1 Samuel 14:49 and 2 Samuel 6:16-23)

For All the Wrong Reasons

Her life began as a princess but ended in jealousy, rage, and dismay.

"Now as the ark of the Lord came into the City of David, Michal, Saul's daughter, looked through a window and saw King David leaping and whirling before the Lord; and she despised him in her heart.
"So they brought the ark of the Lord, and set it in its place in the midst of the tabernacle that David had erected for it. Then David offered burnt offerings and peace offerings before the Lord.
"And when David had finished offering burnt offerings and peace offerings, he blessed the people in the name of the Lord of hosts. Then he distributed among all the people, among the whole multitude

of Israel, both the women and the men, to everyone a loaf of bread, a piece of meat, and a cake of raisins. So all the people departed, everyone to his house.
"Then David returned to bless his household. And Michal the daughter of Saul came out to meet David, and said, 'How glorious was the king of Israel today, uncovering himself today in the eyes of the maids of his servants, as one of the base fellows shamelessly uncovers himself!'
"So David said to Michal, 'It was before the Lord, who chose me instead of your father and all his house, to appoint me ruler over the people of the Lord, over Israel. Therefore, I will play music before the Lord. And I will be even more undignified than this and will be humble in my own sight. But as for the maidservants of whom you have spoken, by them I will be held in honor.'
"Therefore, Michal, the daughter of Saul, had no children to the day of her death."
(2 Samuel 6:16-23 NKJV)

You've already noticed her name: Michal. She's mentioned between 1 Samuel 14:49 and 2 Samuel 6:23. That might seem like a *lot,* covering 620 verses and about 21,358 words. But her *story* is told in just eight verses, using around 190 words. (For reference, you've already read 342 words in this chapter.) It's only a small part of the bigger story, and not much is known about her, but from these eight verses and 190 words, it's clear that Michal was no ordinary girl.

WHO'S THAT GIRL?

Her father was King Saul, Israel's first monarch. He was a man from the tribe of Benjamin and was chosen by God through the prophet Samuel to lead His people when Israel demanded a king. Although God's original plan was for His people not to have a king—He wanted to rule them directly, guiding and protecting them—Saul was divinely appointed to this role when they wanted to be like other nations.

He began his reign with great strength, and under his leadership, Israel achieved notable victories. He succeeded in uniting the different tribes of Israel and experienced significant military success. However, ultimately, it was his disobedience to God that led to his rejection as king. God would choose someone to replace Saul. 1 Samuel 14:49 tells us that he had five children—three sons and two daughters. Michal was the youngest.

Many young girls dream of being a princess. Disney has fostered this desire through the many characters they've created in their franchise. Their stories are full of glamour, excitement, and the pursuit of "happily ever after." However, these fairy tales might give us a false idea of what it was really like to be a princess during Michal's time.

A king's main goal was to produce heirs—sons—to carry on his family's rule. This was the only way to keep his family on the throne. If there were no sons from a legitimate marriage, the crown would pass to the oldest male relative, such as a brother, an uncle, or even a cousin. That's why having a son was so essential for any king.

Royal daughters, though not as celebrated as their sons, still held importance. Due to their royal heritage, they could be used to form strategic alliances, strengthen ties between kingdoms, promote peace and economic stability through marriage, and provide mutual defense. Sadly, daughters of kings often served as bargaining tools, carrying the heavy burden of representing their families' and kingdoms' interests. The same was true for Michal.

NOT JUST ANOTHER HALLMARK MOVIE

David entered the story in 1 Samuel 16. God rejected King Saul because of his disobedience, and Samuel was told to find and anoint the future king. This led him to Jesse's house, where he met the shepherd boy David, and God said, "That's my man!" So, Samuel anointed David with oil, and God began to work powerfully in his life. People saw the evidence of God's blessing

on him, and they started to praise him. "This was their song: 'Saul has killed his thousands, and David his ten thousands!' " (1 Samuel 18:7 NLT)

Saul noticed the praise. Feeling threatened, he began to plan how to eliminate David, and Michal unwittingly became involved in the scheme.

Seeing David as a threat to his throne, he arranged for him to marry his youngest daughter, Michal. After Goliath's death, he offered his older daughter, Merab, to David as a wife. David felt unworthy of this honor, so Merab was given to a man named Adriel instead (see 1 Samuel 18:17-19). With Merab out of the picture, the stage was set for David and Michal's love story to begin.

"In the meantime, Saul's daughter Michal had fallen in love with David. . . ." (1 Samuel 18:20a NLT).

When King Saul realized this, he was pleased because it was a

"chance to see him killed by the Philistines!" (1 Samuel 18:21 NLT).

That's a strange thing to feel happy about. That's not a typical reaction—to take pleasure in the thought that someone might be killed. Saul was so overcome with insecurity that it corrupted his heart and mind. The ugliness of the comparison game was fully on display.

Let's take a moment to pause here. Most people have felt insecure at some point. It's probably safe to say that we've all been tempted to compare our lives and ourselves to others. This tendency often comes from a desire for self-evaluation or self-improvement; however, it can lead to low self-esteem, negative feelings, and even resentment. That's why we're encouraged in Galatians 6:4 to

"Pay careful attention to your own work, for then you will get the satisfaction of a job well done, and you won't need to compare yourself to anyone else." (NLT)

This has been a difficult lesson for me (Billy) to learn. I've always struggled with comparing myself to others. Usually, I compared myself to those I thought were better—like they sang better, looked better, were smarter, or were more committed Christians. Sadly, there were times when I compared myself to those I felt were worse off just to feel better about myself. Living that way is a sad cycle—constantly playing the comparison game. The truth is that this kind of game is a losing one.

Comparing ourselves to others can lead to anxiety, depression, broken relationships, loss of motivation, and it can distract us from the beautiful journey that God has uniquely planned for us. These thoughts and feelings might seem harmless, but they can become dangerous. That's what happened to King Saul!

The Psalmist reminds us that we are **"fearfully and wonderfully made,"** and that God's works (that's us), **"are wonderful." (Psalm 139:14 NIV)**

There's freedom when we begin to realize how special we are to Him and that He has a purpose for each of us. There's no need to compare.

God made them, *them*.

God made you, *you*.

And He made me, *me*.

Let's be who He created us to be!

Now, where were we?

Saul arranged for Michal to marry David because it would be a way to have him killed by the Philistines. *What?* How could that be possible? Remember, David was a shepherd boy. He didn't come from a wealthy family. He even questioned Saul's men after the offer of marriage:

". . . How can a poor man from a humble family afford the bride price for the daughter of a king?" (1 Samuel 18:23 NLT)

That's the point: if David married the princess and became the king's son-in-law, a bride price would need to be paid—an amount or gift from the groom to the bride's family at marriage. Think of it as a dowry, just reversed. It didn't mean the groom was buying the bride; it was a way to establish a covenant between the two families. Ultimately, it was a sign of serious commitment by the groom and a demonstration of his ability to care for his future wife. What would the price be if David became the king's son-in-law? King Saul had a plan.

YOU WANT WHAT?

"When Saul's men reported this back to the king, he told them, 'Tell David that all I want for the bride price is 100 Philistine foreskins! Vengeance on my enemies is all I really want.' "
(1 Samuel 18:25 NLT)

The bride price the king demands reveals how jealousy and insecurity affect Saul's life. He has become so insecure that he set a trap for the man he sees as a rival. Think about it: to get rid of David, Saul offered his daughter in exchange for a bride price he believed would be impossible to pay. Remember—the Philistines were fierce warriors.

They've fought Israel many times before. In fact, Goliath was a Philistine, and when Saul and his army cowered, David—with the power of God on his side—stepped up and faced Goliath. Now, if David were to marry Michal, he'd have to face the Philistines them again. This time, he'd battle a whole army of them. Saul thought this would eliminate his rival, but God had a different plan.

"David was delighted to accept the offer. Before the time limit expired, he and his men went out and killed 200 Philistines. Then David fulfilled the king's requirement by presenting all their foreskins to him."
(1 Samuel 18:26-27 NLT)

Here's something that can't be denied: You can't keep God's man down. What seemed like an impossible task, what was a murderous plot, could not stop what God had planned. His will would be fulfilled! There would now be a wedding... the bride price had been doubled. That's great news for Michal, as we're again told of her love for David in 1 Samuel 18:28. (Surprisingly, we don't see any mention of David's love for her.)

However, we also read that

"Saul became even more afraid of him, and he remained David's enemy for the rest of his life."
(1 Samuel 18:29 NLT)

The in-law relationship would not be a good one. In fact, it would lead from one battle to the next, where ultimately Saul would lose his life.

LOVE ON THE LOOSE, HEART ON THE RUN

One murderous plot led to another. We don't have time to cover them all, so let's fast-forward through the rest of 1 Samuel:

- Saul attempts to kill David by throwing a javelin.
- David escapes Saul's next murderous attempt with Michal's help by being lowered out of his own bedroom window.
- Jonathan, Saul's son, warns David about his father's increased efforts to kill him.

- Battle after battle, David remains separated from Michal and keeps living on the run.
- David repeatedly spares Saul's life.
- Michal is married to Palti by her father (1 Samuel 25:44).

It might be surprising to learn that Michal was forced into another marriage by her father. That would be a natural response. But remember that Saul was trying to stay on the throne, so his plan was a political move to cut off the connection between his daughter and his rival. It was meant to eliminate any claim that David had to the throne.

It's hard to imagine the impact this had on Michal. She had been separated from the man she loved (remember 1 Samuel 18:20, 28) and was now forced to be with another man chosen by her father because of his loyalty to the king. But it seemed like Palti loved Michal. (Interestingly, we never read that Michal loved him.) One thing's for sure, Michal's life hadn't been easy. It's probably safe to say that it hadn't always been fun. It was definitely not a fairy tale. Something was happening to her, and we'll see that clearly later in her story.

Long Live the King!

1 Samuel 31 describes Saul's final battle, marking his death and setting the stage for David's rise to the throne. What was foretold long ago came true. Interestingly, David mourned Saul's death after executing the man

who claimed responsibility for Saul's downfall. (Please read the chapter for a complete picture.)

When David was about thirty years old, he became King of Judah and ruled for seven years. Eventually, he was anointed King of the entire nation of Israel. During that time, he also sent for his first wife, Michal. Remember, she'd been married to Palti for years, and he seemed to really care for her. As David's men were bringing Michal back to him, Palti followed weeping—until he was ordered to return home.

There she was, Michal, daughter of Saul. Interestingly, she was identified this way. She wasn't called Michal, David's first wife. She wasn't referred to as Michal, Queen of Israel. Instead, she was consistently known as the "daughter of Saul." That was her main identity.

Let me emphasize a hard reality: life had not been a fairy tale for Michal. It hadn't been easy, nor had it been fun. She'd been used by her own father and had given her heart away at a young age—only to have it broken. She thought she'd found love, but now she was forced to start over. She often seemed to play a minor role in her own story. Something had changed inside her. She had become cold, and it was clear that her marriage to David was just another political move—it served its purpose.

She'd been hardened by life. The butterflies that once made her stomach flutter at the sight of David had disappeared. The love that burned passionately within her had cooled so much that there was barely a flicker left. And now we read she,

". . . despised him in her heart."
(2 Samuel 6:16 NIV)

Let's pause the story and chat again for a moment. When I graduated from college, I began my ministry as a youth pastor just outside Gary, Indiana, in the Chicagoland area. Overall, it was a great experience, but there were also difficult times.

My senior pastor, who was also my boss, was a man named Ron Richmond. He was a great guy, full of energy, and he became like a father to me. (It's a long story, but during my first week there, my father passed away, and Ron stepped into that role.)

One of the challenges I faced as a youth pastor was working with people, especially parents. Youth ministry would be great if you didn't have to deal with parents! Earlier in this chapter, I shared my struggles with playing the comparison game. Another issue I've struggled with is responding appropriately to people when I feel attacked or criticized. I'm sure I wasn't the only youth pastor to face this, but it was a significant challenge.

I'm grateful for Ron's help with this. He always said, "You can't control how people treat you, but you can always control how you respond to them." That's a life lesson I truly value. No one can control everything that happens in life, but we *can* control what happens inside us. We are reminded to

**"Keep our heart with all diligence,
for out of it spring the issues of life."
(Proverbs 4:23 HCSB)**

Life had hardened Michal, and now we see it clearly in 2 Samuel 6:12-23.

SOMEBODY GO GET GOD

The Ark of the Covenant symbolized God's blessing and Presence among His people. It accompanied the Israelites through the desert, leading and representing His divine guidance, provision, and protection. It went into battle with them and helped secure victory for His children. It was the central focus of their worship. Once again, it represented God's blessing and Presence with His people.

Now that David had claimed his rightful place as king of Israel, it was time to bring the Ark to Jerusalem. When David first tried this, he went as a victorious king with a mighty army and ignored God's instructions for transporting the Ark. Do you remember the story of Uzzah? If not, read 2 Samuel 6:1-10a. After Uzzah's death, David questioned how to proceed, decided he couldn't continue, and left the Ark at Obed-Edom's house, where it stayed for three months. Although that wasn't a long time—just a season—God blessed it.

News of this spread to Jerusalem and reached the king's ears. When he learned how God was blessing him, he decided to finish what he had started. But this time, he did it God's way, and a worship celebration broke out. David danced before the Lord. The people danced before the Lord. Everyone celebrated as the Ark entered the city—everyone except her:

"As the ark of the Lord was entering the City of David, Michal, daughter of Saul watched from a window. And when she saw King David leaping and dancing before the Lord, she despised him in her heart."
(2 Samuel 6:16 NIV)

She sat in her tower, watching what was happening outside her window. They all enjoyed the presence of God, and she looked down on them.

The celebration resulted in blessings:

"Then he gave a loaf of bread, a cake of dates and a cake of raisins to each person in the whole crowd of Israelites, both men and women. And all the people went to their homes.
(2 Samuel 6:19 NIV)

There's a powerful lesson for us to learn from this: When God is in His rightful place, everybody benefits.

When God is in His rightful place in government, the nation benefits. When He's given His proper place in the home, the family benefits. If He were to have His proper place in church, the entire congregation would benefit. It's such a powerful picture. Have you given Him His rightful place in your life? David had brought the Ark back to His people, and they all benefited.

Having blessed all the people of Israel, David now intends to bring the blessing to his own household. Sadly, before he even entered the palace, Michal came out and stopped the blessing. Look at verse 20:

"Then David returned to bless his household. And Michal the daughter of Saul came out to meet David, and said, 'How glorious was the king of Israel today, uncovering himself today in the eyes of the maids of his servants, as one of the base fellows shamelessly uncovers himself!' " (2 Samuel 6:20 NKJV)

Michal stopped the blessing!

Do you realize it's possible to block God's blessings? When we choose our way over His, we hinder what He wants to do. It's incredible that an all-powerful God, in whom nothing is impossible, has limited Himself by our responses. May it never be that, by insisting things happen my way, I block what He wants to do. Michal did. And, honestly, you can hear the hurt from her past.

(Did you catch the remark about the maidservants?) There's insecurity there, in herself. But we are called to find our security in Him.

When the story ends, this is what we read:

"Therefore Michal the daughter of Saul had no children to the day of her death." (2 Samuel 6:23 NKJV)

"Therefore" is a conjunctive adverb. It shows a conclusion or a result in a story. You can also think of it as a connecting word. In other words, what follows is a result of what you've already read.

Based on what we've read and what we've seen through her actions—Michal remained childless. She had no children; she was barren. Throughout her life, she produced no offspring. That's the last detail we know about her. After 2 Samuel 6:23, Michal disappeared from the pages of history.

She was never mentioned again in Scripture.

There was nothing more.

And we remember her for all the wrong reasons.

ONE LAST THING

Michal's story has been written; however, ours is still being composed. We can learn from her mistakes. Bitterness and a critical spirit have destructive effects. They steal joy and lead to isolation and spiritual death.

When we hold conflicting loyalties, we risk prioritizing human relationships over our connection with God.

Michal's life warns us how anger and resentment can cause personal and spiritual emptiness. We may find ourselves not only isolated from others but also separated from God, causing our spiritual life to become lifeless and barren. So, let's keep God in His proper place and live a meaningful story. Our endings are still being written.

GOING DEEPER

- **Have you ever found yourself playing the comparison game? How did it impact your feelings? What helped you to stop?**
- **How do you handle difficult people? Is there an example you're willing to share about how you responded the wrong way or the right way? How did each experience make you feel?**
- **What insights can you share about Michal's life? Are there aspects you relate to? What are your personal feelings about her story?**
- **Can you share an example of how your spiritual life has flourished or stalled because of decisions you've made?**

When we choose our way over His, we hinder what He wants to do.

Playing the comparison game is always a losing battle.

When God is in His rightful place, everybody benefits.

Here's something that can't be denied: You can't keep God's man down.

ONE-HIT WONDER: GARY DAHL

The year was 1975. Gary Dahl had a job in advertising, and as a joke, he created what's known as the "Pet Rock." He wrote advertising copy to go along with it, created a carrying box and even included "instructions" on how to care for your pet rock.

For a mere three dollars and 95 cents, anyone could buy—a rock—a plain, ordinary, egg-shaped rock—something you could dig up in almost any backyard. Almost immediately after its invention, more than a million people purchased the Pet Rock and bragged about owning one.

Newsweek magazine later called it "one of the most ridiculously successful marketing schemes ever." Gary Dahl, made more than a million dollars on his invention.

What happened next? We don't really know. He passed away in 2015 as a one-hit wonder.

CHAPTER THIRTEEN

(Mark 12:41-45)

She Didn't Know

Because she gave what little she had,
her story is still being told centuries later.
And we don't even know her name.

"Beware of the scribes, who desire to go around in long robes, love greetings in the marketplaces, the best seats in the synagogues, and the best places at feasts, who devour widows' houses, and for a pretense make long prayers. These will receive greater condemnation." (Mark 12:38-40 NKJV)

Jesus warned His listeners in the temple on Tuesday about a whirlwind week. It began on Sunday when Jesus willingly entered Jerusalem. That was truly remarkable. The one place He should have avoided—the exact place His enemies were waiting—He humbly made His entrance.

He wasn't forced by whips and chains, nor was He dragged kicking and screaming. It certainly wasn't the imagery of a conquering King seated proudly upon a muscular stallion, as Jesus was seated upon a donkey's colt.

The crowds had gathered in Jerusalem to begin the Passover week celebration—nearly 2.5 million devout Jewish people were present. They were busy with their religious routines, focused on choosing their Passover lamb. They did this to remember what God had done during the exodus many years earlier. It was also celebrated with hope, trusting that God would send the Messiah to renew the exodus and bring freedom to His people. While they were engaged in religious activities, God was doing something new. God was sending *His* Lamb. The question that needed to be answered—Will you choose My Lamb?

As they saw Jesus descending the mountain, they remembered the words of the prophet and hurried out to greet him, waving palm branches and shouting, "Hosanna!" As the excitement reached its peak, Jesus rode heartbroken on the back of that donkey. He heard their cries, but He knew their hearts. This Passover would change everything. As Sunday turned into Monday, the whirlwind grew more intense.

The day began with Jesus cursing a fig tree as He was heading to the Temple. It was a confusing yet powerful scene symbolizing the coming judgment of Israel for its lack of fruitfulness. When Monday afternoon arrived, it was loud with Jesus as He cleared the temple:

"Is it not written, 'My house shall be called a house of prayer for all nations'? But you have made it a den of thieves.' "
(Mark 11:17 NKJV)

This ultimately led to His own judgment by the religious leaders, who now

". . . sought how they might destroy Him. . ."
(Mark 11:18 NKJV)

As the day ended, Jesus left the city but planned to return on Tuesday.

Tuesday was filled with questions. It could be called a time of inquisition. The interrogation came from every side. The chief priests, scribes, and elders asked, *"Who gave you the authority to do these things?"* Then came the Pharisees and Herodians asking, *"Is it lawful to pay taxes to Caesar or not?"* And, not to be outdone, the Sadducees had to get their question in, *"At the resurrection, whose wife will she be, since there were 7 husbands?"* (By the way, the Sadducees didn't even believe in the resurrection or the afterlife!)

All these games prompted Jesus to issue a warning—Woe to you! Depending on which gospel you read, He called them: blind guides, hypocrites, whitewashed tombs, dens of snakes, brood of vipers, you who strain at a gnat but swallow a camel. He didn't hold back. Jesus was definitely descriptive!

Then we hear His broken heart as He laments:

"Jerusalem, Jerusalem, you who kill the prophets and stone those sent to you, how often I have longed to gather you as a hen gathers her chicks under her wings, and you were not willing. Look, your house is left to you desolate. For I tell you, you will not see me again until you say, 'Blessed is he who comes in the name of the Lord.' "
(Matthew 23:37-39 NIV)

They made their choice and rejected the Lamb of God, and Jesus was heartbroken. It was against this backdrop that the warning against the scribes was given. With this Lament, Jesus' public ministry ended.

"Now Jesus sat opposite the treasury and saw how the people put money into the treasury. And many *who were* rich put in much."
(Mark 12:41 NKJV)

It had been a long and exhausting few days, with Tuesday being especially tough. Now, Jesus needed rest—physically, mentally, and emotionally. Surrounded by the large holiday crowd, it would've been easy to blend in, so He headed just outside the "Court of the Women" to where offerings were made. God had commanded His people back in Exodus to bring offerings for the good of the Temple as a form of worship, and that tradition continued in the Herodian Temple. Here, directly across from the treasury, Jesus found a quiet spot to sit not far from the "Beautiful Gate," which overlooks the Mount of Olives. Usually, it would've been a peaceful scene, but with all the holiday visitors and activity around the offerings, it was anything but peaceful.

There were thirteen receptacles for temple guests to make offerings, commonly called "trumpets" or "chests." They received this name because of their shape: trumpet-shaped, with a narrow opening at the top and a wider, chest-like base. Each was designated for a specific type of offering.

There was one for the present and previous censuses (see Exodus 30:13), four were meant to support the sacrifices, one for the mercy seat, and six for freewill offerings. The offering time had become a spectacle. Because of the trumpet-shaped offering jars, the coins would rattle against the sides as they were put in, making loud noises. The larger the donation, the louder the sound. The louder the noise, the higher the risk of pride. That's why Jesus warned,

"So when you give, do not announce it with trumpets, as the hypocrites do. . . ."
(Matthew 6:2 NIV)

While everyone watched what was happening in the treasury, Jesus sat against the wall. From this position, all eyes wouldn't be on Him, allowing Him to observe quietly. A woman was blending into the crowd that day…

"Then a poor widow came and dropped in two small coins." (Mark 12:42 NLT)

She went unnoticed.

She was without a name.

She appeared to be insignificant.

But—she had His attention.

Let's pause for a moment and step outside our story. There are many times in life when we can relate to this woman. The world is filled with people. In fact, a quick Google search shows that in 2023, there were 8.062 billion people, and the United Nations Population Fund predicts that by 2037, the global population will reach 9 billion, increasing to an incredible 10 billion by 2058. I'll say it again: the world is full of people! It's easy to get lost in a crowd like that.

There are many individuals doing countless things. When we see their success and fame, it's easy to feel invisible, unnamed, and very small. Our lives can seem so tiny. We wonder if we're making a difference, if our efforts matter at all, or if anyone notices or cares. Maybe, even now, you're feeling those same emotions while reading this. So, before we go any further, remember this: Nothing goes unnoticed with Jesus. You have His attention, and so does the woman in this story.

While many wealthy people threw in a lot—causing a loud noise to echo through the treasury—she quietly made her way to the "trumpet" clutching her two small coins in her hands.

Two. Small. Coins.

Pause!

Let's step out of the story once more. We must.

There are times while reading the Bible when the action unfolds as we expect. For example, when we hear about the questioning Jesus faced earlier in the inquiry, we know the questioners won't gain the upper hand. We expect that, so the story continues as anticipated.

Then, there are other moments when Jesus surprises us by doing something unexpected. (I like to say, just when you think you know Jesus, He goes and does something surprising!) This is one of those times.

When we consider the scene, He should have stopped her.

Why?

I'll give a few reasons.

HE SHOULD HAVE STOPPED HER

#1: Consider WHO she was

The description given is very brief: one poor widow. That's it. Three words that speak volumes. In biblical times, losing a husband was not only an emotional tragedy but also a social and economic one. In a male-dominated culture, the death of a husband was like a cultural death for the widow.

Now, she would live a marginal existence, often in extreme poverty. Don't misunderstand—widows did have a place in ancient Jewish society, but it was not a prominent one. She wouldn't hold a position of influence, especially since she was *poor*.

This classification would have put her alongside orphans and migrants. Her life would be one of dependence on others. According to the law, she might be gleaning figs at dawn or, at dusk, probably mixed with migrants gathering grain on the edges of fields. In her vulnerable state, she could have offered her services to help others with daily chores: cleaning, cooking, or even sewing.

Because of their vulnerable position, widows were easily exploited and abused, but she would do whatever she could to regain some of the security she lost with her husband's death. There she was—a woman trying to make it in a man's world—clutching her offering. He should have stopped her.

#2: Consider WHAT she gave.

She gave two small coins. These coins, depending on the translation of the Bible, are called by different names.

They're called a *lepton*, a *prutah*, or a *mite*—two tiny coins. What were they? They were the smallest denomination of currency used during those times. In today's terms, they would be worth about 1/8 of a cent.

But when she made her offering, the combined value of the two coins would equal 1/64 of a common laborer's daily wage. In other words, it was roughly what an average worker earns in about 12 minutes of work. Read that again: *12 minutes* of a day's pay.

She was there among the millions in Jerusalem, in line at the temple treasury, holding her 12 minutes' worth of pay, as "many who were rich put in much" (v41).

What good could two small coins possibly do? To her, they would be more valuable than to the temple. As the trumpets sounded with the offerings, hers would barely make a clink, clank, or toot.

Would anybody hear?

Would anybody care?

Probably not . . . but Jesus heard, and that's why He probably should have stopped her.

#3: Consider WHERE she was.

We'll divide this into two categories: *who* she was giving to and *what* she was giving. First, who was she giving to? Simply put—the religious establishment. They were the ones Jesus warned His listeners about earlier that day. Do you remember His warning?

"Beware of the scribes,
who desire to go around in long robes,
love greetings in the marketplaces,
the best seats in the synagogues,
and the best places at feasts. . . ."
(Mark 12:38-39 NKJV)

Her two small coins would go to those who were self-important, longed for a life of leisure and privilege, wanted recognition, and loved to be seen. Their arrogance knew no bounds, and their pride was unmatched. His warning doesn't end there; Jesus continues,

"who devour widows' houses,
and for a pretense make long prayers.
These will receive greater condemnation."
(Mark 12:40 NKJV)

Read that again: who devour widows' houses.

One more time:

WHO.

DEVOUR.

WIDOWS'.

HOUSES.

This is a powerful indictment! These self-serving, egomaniacs exploit their position and privilege to abuse, overwhelm, and *completely consume* (that's the meaning of the Greek term *katesthiontes* [*devour*]) widows' houses. Jesus uses very strong, graphic language to describe how they take advantage of people like her, a poor widow. That's *who* she was giving to.

Then, think about what her two small coins could support—a corrupt temple system. It was only Monday when Jesus drove out the money changers, exclaiming,

"you have made it a den of thieves."
(see Mark 11:17 NKJV)

Sadly, the temple had become a symbol of the religious leaders' pride and hypocrisy, used to extort people for their own benefit. Fast forward past this scene, and Jesus will predict its destruction.

"As Jesus was leaving the Temple that day, one of His disciples said, 'Teacher, look at these magnificent buildings! Look at the impressive stones in the walls.'
"Jesus replied, 'Yes, look at these great buildings. But they will be completely demolished. Not one stone will be left on top of another!' "
(Mark 13:1-2 NLT)

That's what Jesus predicted, and in 70 AD, just 37 years later, the prophecy came true when the Romans destroyed Jerusalem. During the five-month siege, they burned the temple, causing the leftover gold to melt into the cracks of the masonry and the great stones. They tore down the structure piece by piece, stone by stone, leaving only a level foundation. And that's what she was giving to. Isn't it obvious now? He really should have stopped her. I know I would have, wouldn't you?

But He didn't. Instead, he watched as she gave the most beautiful offering.

THE MOST BEAUTIFUL OFFERING

Unnoticed.

Unnamed.

Insignificant.

But His eyes watched her as she loosened her grip on her two small coins. As she extended her arm to the trumpet to drop them in, Jesus called for His disciples and said,

"I tell you the truth, this poor widow has given more than all the others who are making contributions. For they gave a tiny part of their surplus, but she, poor as she is, has given everything she had to live on."
(Mark 12:43-44 NLT)

This is what it's all about! Three years of the disciples' journey with Jesus is captured in a moment in time:" . . . *she, as poor as she is, has given everything she had to live on."* While many who had much to give contributed from their riches, she gave all she had to sustain herself. The Greek root *bios* is used here, from which we get our English word *biology*, meaning "the science of life."

When she gave everything she had to live on—that meant just that. She loosened her grip on all the means by which her life was sustained. All that she possessed, she gave away without expecting anything in return. There were no strings attached. She had no desire for a thank you.

There was no expectation or demand for anything in return. Unnoticed by everyone else, she simply surrendered all the stuff of life as an act of service to her God. Her gift may not have meant much to the temple, the religious community, or anyone else, but it meant everything to Him! Not because her offering would support the work of the temple or religious establishment. Instead, it revealed her faith that God would support her.

There's nothing more beautiful than a person who's willing to trust God with everything—every part of life. There's nothing more precious to Him than a woman who entrusts her care to the God in whom she believes and trusts. There's no greater lesson we can learn than this: It's safe to trust Him!

Do you know that?

Has that happened in your life?

IT'S SAFE TO TRUST HIM

While writing this chapter, I (Billy) was conducting revival services at the Pleasant View Church of the Nazarene in Jamestown, Tenn. Things started off great on Sunday, and I was excited for the Monday evening service. I was staying at an Airbnb about four miles from the church. When I arrived for that service, my car's engine began to miss badly. If you've ever experienced something like this, you understand the anxiety it causes.

On Tuesday, I found out that my eight-cylinder engine had decided to become a seven-cylinder. My car would stay in the shop until Thursday morning. Car repairs aren't cheap, and an unexpected bill of any amount can be a big inconvenience. I was involved in several projects that limited my finances at the time, but I had to have my vehicle.

Tuesday night service arrived, and the pastor surprised me by mentioning my car troubles and taking up a special offering. (I hadn't mentioned it to anyone except him.) When I got back to the Airbnb, I found that the amount was right around what the mechanic had quoted.

I slept peacefully that night, confident that everything would work out. However, that all changed the next morning when he called and said there were some additional repairs needed that would almost double the cost. I was still relieved I wouldn't have to cover the entire expense myself, but now there was that unexpected charge.

Wednesday evening after the service, there were two people who couldn't participate in the offering the night before but handed me their donations. Also, I realized I had forgotten a check that a supporter of my ministry had given me before the Tuesday service. When I went to get my vehicle on Thursday, I had the exact amount for the repair, with about $0.26 to spare. I was reminded that it's safe to trust Him with all the stuff of life. He just never fails to provide for His own!

Page after page could be filled with records of His faithfulness in our lives. Maybe you should take a moment (or two) to remember how He has been faithful to you. We all need to reflect on this from time to time.

SHE DIDN'T EVEN KNOW

On Tuesday of Passover week, as the days quickly approached Friday when Jesus would offer His life, the most costly of sacrifices, He paused and noticed her and her offering worth less than a cent. No one else noticed. Perhaps no one else cared. But Jesus did, and He pointed her out to His disciples. Now, her story is recorded for all generations to read.

Unnoticed?

Unnamed?

Insignificant?

Not really.
At least not anymore.
She was a hit, a wonder.
And she didn't even know it!

THE APPLAUSE OF HEAVEN

I can't help but wonder what it must have been like when she arrived in Heaven. Did countless people approach her and exclaim, "You're the one! I know your story!"

You may feel as though you are

Unnoticed.

Unnamed.

Insignificant.

Maybe it seems like all your efforts are meaningless and not making a difference or having an impact. During those times, remember her story and realize that He notices you, He knows your name, and whatever you do in His name holds eternal significance. One day soon, you too will hear the applause of heaven!

I'm so glad He didn't stop her.

Aren't you?

GOING DEEPER

- Have you ever felt unnoticed? That your work or ministry seemed unimportant? How did you get through those moments?
- Reflecting on the last question and answer, have you ever overlooked the work or ministry that someone else was involved in? What actions can you take in the future to stay aware and show gratitude and appreciation for others' efforts?
- Was there a moment in your Christian life when you had to fully trust in Jesus and depend on Him for the outcome? What was that moment, and how did He bring about the solution? Also, how important do you think it is to share those experiences with others? Why?
- Would you have stopped the widow?

Nothing goes unnoticed with Jesus.

They made their choice and rejected the Lamb of God, and Jesus was heartbroken.

God was doing something new. God was sending His Lamb.

ONE-HIT WONDER: XAVIER ROBERTS

CABBAGE PATCH DOLLS

It was 1976 and Xavier Roberts was a 21-year-old art student when he came up with the beginning Cabbage Patch Kids doll. By 1978, Xavier recruited five of his school friends and started a company that sold the entirely plush, hand-made at a retail price of $100.

He traveled to art and craft shows to sell his dolls, which already had the signature adoption aspect to them. By 1983, the dolls were 16-inches tall, with a plastic head, a fabric body, and yarn hair (unless it was bald).

What made them so desirable, besides the fact that they were huggable, was both their supposed uniqueness and their "adoptability."

It was claimed that each Cabbage Patch Kids doll was unique. Different head molds, eye shapes and eye colors, hairstyles and hair colors, and clothing options made each one look different than the other. This, plus the fact that inside each Cabbage Patch Kids box came a "birth certificate" with that particular doll's first and middle name on it, made the dolls as individual as the children who wanted to adopt them.

Xavier later sold his invention to Mattel toy company, and they dropped the size of the doll from 16 inches to 14 inches. Whatever happened to Xavier Roberts? Well, since making a fortune from Cabbage Patch Kids, he has stayed out of the spotlight. He was definitely a one-hit wonder!

CHAPTER FOURTEEN

(Mark 15:21)

In the Spotlight

Some one-hit wonders seek the spotlight of fame, and others accidentally wander onto the stage. But this man was literally forced into the spotlight.

Millions of people throughout history have worked hard and fought to be remembered in history books, but Simon of Cyrene was *thrown* into the pages of history. Except for one event in his life, he might have remained unknown, but because of that one experience, his name is recognized worldwide wherever the Gospel of Jesus is known.

There's not much said about Simon in the Bible. In fact, just about everything we know about him is found in Mark 15:21, and in one verse in each of the Gospels of Matthew and Luke, which are parallels of this one. Let's take a look:

**"There was a man walking by,
coming from work, Simon from Cyrene,
the father of Alexander and Rufus.
They made him carry Jesus' cross."
(Mark 15:21 The Message)**

This doesn't tell us much. A little research shows he worked in the country. When Jesus falls from the weight of the Cross—after being brutally tortured far beyond what was legal—the officials FORCE Simon to carry Jesus' cross.

What DO we know about Simon of Cyrene.

#1:
WE KNOW WHERE HE WAS FROM AND WHAT HE WAS DOING.

He was from Cyrene, one of the two largest towns in Libya, North Africa, with a population of over 100,000. It was a city with many Jewish residents, and a large number of them would travel all the way to Jerusalem for Passover and Pentecost. Simon was a devout believer in God—as were many Jews in his area.

He was willing to travel more than a thousand miles to Jerusalem to worship at the temple. But what he was doing when he was suddenly—in a moment—forced to change the entire direction of his life? Was he simply passing by? He knew nothing of all that had happened in the city the previous night. Jesus had been going through the agonies of Gethsemane, the trial, and had endured the cruel mocking and beatings of the mob and soldiers.

He was probably exhausted.

Simon had no doubt been sleeping. He had a long day ahead, and as was typical for all Orthodox Jews, he was up early in the morning to say his prayers. He was dressed, cleaned, and almost reached the city before 9 a.m.

If he had arrived three minutes earlier or three minutes later, or if he'd taken a different route, we would've never heard of him. But in God's providence, Simon was to have an experience that morning that changed his entire life. This brings us to the second thing we know about Simon.

#2:
WE KNOW HE WAS FORCED TO CARRY THE CROSS OF CHRIST.

As Simon approached the city gate, he saw a crowd coming out of the city. They were shouting and mocking three men who were carrying crosses. One of them was struggling, and it was obvious he was holding up the procession.

The soldiers, eager to complete their task, ordered Simon to carry Jesus' cross. The Roman soldiers had the authority to force a civilian to help them. Why they chose Simon is unknown. We *do* know that Jesus had been up all night and had taken a beating known to have killed other men. So, it's easy to understand that Jesus stumbled and fell under the load.

Simon was probably the only one in the crowd *not* mocking Jesus, making him a likely choice.

UNPLANNED MEETING

Simon was on his way to church when he found himself in a crucifixion parade. Just touching the cross would have contaminated him, ruining his day. What a miserable way to meet the Master. He probably felt the blood of Jesus and even touched His broken body on the day Jesus died. Simon's unique experience probably moved him from simply believing in God to placing his faith in Jesus Himself.

He was on his way to worship God when he was interrupted by the need to help Christ carry the cross to redeem the world. Of course, he didn't realize what was happening. He traveled a thousand miles to do something meaningful, and by carrying the cross, he ended up playing a part in helping to save the world.

Simon did *not* rebel at this sudden turn of events. Like Lydia and others who were honestly seeking to know the will of God, he had, no doubt, prayed that very morning, "Lord teach me Thy will, and draw me closer to You this day."

He had traveled a great distance (a thousand miles from Cyrene to Jerusalem) searching for a deeper understanding of God, so he endured the shame of carrying the cross. He was forced to bear it, but he chose to submit.

The fact that nothing more is said indicates that Simon didn't resist, but bore the cross without a struggle. If only we, like Simon, would choose to bear what we're compelled to bear. Circumstances compel us to bear burdens, but we can choose to submit or rebel.

This principle is true for all of life. For example, young people are required to go to school. Many wouldn't choose this if they had the option. But since we're forced to go, we have two choices. We can rebel and fight the system, quitting as soon as possible, or we can see it as a challenge, decide to accept the burden, and watch it turn into a blessing. We can't determine what life brings to us, but we can determine what we bring to life. And if we choose to do what we're compelled to do, we can change burdens into blessings. The third thing we know about Simon is this:

#3. WE UNDERSTAND THE CONSEQUENCES OF HIS BEARING CHRIST'S CROSS.

It's also certain that, although the cross kept Simon from a church service that morning, it brought him to Christ. Our Scripture states that Simon was the father of Alexander and Rufus. Let's review it again:

"A certain man from Cyrene, Simon, the father of Alexander and Rufus, was passing by on his way in from the country, and they forced him to carry the cross." (Mark 15:21 NIV)

Just as we don't know much about Simon, we also don't know much about his sons. We know they were clearly old enough to take this 1,000-mile trip with their dad. So, they were probably in their early 20s.

Why would Mark, who wrote his Gospel account for the Roman audience, mention that Simon was the father of Alexander and Rufus unless these two young men were known to the Romans? There seems to be no point in including these names unless they were familiar to the Roman believers, right?

Simon's two sons' names wouldn't be known if Simon had simply disappeared into the crowd after reaching Golgotha. The other Gospels *don't* mention the names of these two sons. This suggests that, by the time Mark wrote *his* Gospel account, these two sons of Simon were well-known Christians in Rome. This is even confirmed by Paul in his letter to the Romans, where he says:

"I send greetings to Rufus, that outstanding worker in the Lord's service, and to his mother, who has always treated me like a son."
(Romans 16:13 GNT)

Where did this remarkable Christian family originate? Paul hadn't been to Rome when he wrote his letter, so he must have met them *before* they relocat*ed* there. By combining all these facts, we see that Simon of Cyrene was the first convert from Africa. He returned to his home and led his family to Christ. From there, they probably moved to Antioch. But how do we know THIS?

Because of what we read in Acts 13:1, we learn about the prophets and teachers there, two of whom were Simon and Lucius of Cyrene. It was here—in Antioch—where the followers of Jesus were first called Christians. Who knows how much he who carried the cross of Christ had to do with that! He was the first convert at the cross and became a leader where believers were first called Christians.

It was *here* that Paul would get to know the family and later speak of them when they moved to Rome—as we just read in Romans 16:13. There's much we don't know, but these facts teach us that although Simon was forced to carry the cross for a short time by the soldiers, he CHOSE to carry it for the rest of his life for the Savior. This one-hit wonder is making a lasting impact!

There's one more thing we know about Simon.

#4. WE KNOW HIS EXPERIENCE WAS RECORDED FOR A PURPOSE.

We're told that all Scripture is given by inspiration of God and is profitable. Here's the proof:

"The whole Bible was given to us by inspiration from God and is useful to teach us what is true." (2 Timothy 3:16 MEV)

So, we know Simon's story—though very brief—is included in the Bible for a reason. It teaches us what it really means to bear the cross. Today, the cross has become for many people nothing more than a piece of jewelry.

We wear golden crosses around our necks or on our lapels as decorations. There's nothing wrong with the cross as a symbol like this, but there's something wrong with our thinking about it.

The experience of Simon teaches us to think of the cross as an identification with Christ, and not merely a decoration. When Simon bore the cross of Christ, he became identified with Christ. Jesus said,

"Whoever wants to be my disciple must deny themselves and take up their cross daily and follow me."
(Luke 9:23 NIV)

That means openly identifying with Jesus, and if people mock Christ, they'll mock you. That's why it's not as easy to talk about Jesus as it is about the weather or politics. In some groups, it's embarrassing and difficult to be associated with Christ. Simon may have felt ashamed as he picked up the cross and heard the laughter and mockery of the crowd.

Bearing the Cross is not the same kind of suffering caused by injury or weakness in the body. That's a thorn, not a cross. The cross is *only* taken up when we are so closely identified with Christ that others will feel and act toward us as they do toward Him. If someone loves Jesus, they will also love you. If someone despises Jesus, they will also despise you. This means that Christ expects us every day to be so united with Him that it costs us to be a Christian.

FOLLOWING JESUS COSTS

There was an American tourist group visiting the Holy Land. One of their stops was Jerusalem. They wanted to walk the path that Jesus took on His way to the cross. It was hot that day, and the leader had an umbrella over his head to shield him from the blazing sun.

One of the group members noticed to himself the striking contrast between this and the real incident. They wanted to follow the path of Christ—but did NOT want any discomfort in doing so.

It's understandable—after all—they wouldn't gain anything from being miserable while following the path. But when this philosophy extends into the spiritual realm, it becomes tragic. We want to follow Jesus, but we don't want it to cost anything.

A man from India shared with a group of Americans what it cost him to follow Christ. He first heard the call of Christ in a Methodist church in Madras. He came from a Brahmin family, and his father was the community's leader.

When his father learned of his decision for Christ, he exploded with anger. He tied him to a pillar in the courtyard of his home. He stripped the turban from his head—a mark of shame in the East—and whipped his back until blood flowed, then made him stand in the hot sun for hours.

They even poured the contents of the sewage bin over his head. They branded him with two large scars on his face using red-hot irons. His own mother died of shock before him. His sister finally freed him, and he fled to the hills.

He eventually became a chaplain in the army. Many have suffered similar consequences for crimes, but when it's endured because one is identified with Christ, that's cross-bearing.

Simon of Cyrene was a one-hit wonder, but the lessons from his story still TEACH us—centuries later. The story of Simon is recorded for the purpose of challenging each of us to take up the cross and be identified with Jesus whatever the cost.

GOING DEEPER

- **It's easy to be a Christian if we don't bear the cross. But is that *genuine* Christianity?**
- **How would you have reacted if you were in Simon's sandals that day and the cross had been thrust into *your* hands?**
- **Identify a time when it has been difficult for you to identify with Christ among your peers.**
- **Recall a time when you took a stand for Christ even though it was difficult to do so.**

Christ expects us every day to be so identified with Him that it costs us to be a Christian.

We can't determine what life brings to us, but we can determine what we bring to life.

It was here—in Antioch—where the followers of Jesus were first called Christians.

He was forced to bear it, but he chose to submit.

ONE-HIT WONDER:
TIM BERNERS-LEE

WWW

Tim, originally from London, graduated with a physics degree from Queen's College at Oxford in 1973. He then worked as an engineer for Plessey, a telecommunications company, before taking on a variety of roles, including working as an independent contractor for CERN.

In 1980, Tim conceived the idea for the World Wide Web. His concepts emerged from exploring hypertext and connecting it to domain name systems.

While all of these ideas existed, Tim was the first to combine and experiment with them, ultimately creating the World Wide Web.

CHAPTER FIFTEEN

(2 Kings 22:12-20)

A Stranger in Her Own World

Have you ever felt lonely in a crowd? It's likely Huldah understood this feeling deeply.

"Go, inquire of the Lord for me,
for the people and for all of Judah,
concerning the words of this
book that has been found. . . ."
(2 Kings 22:13 NKJV)

Those were the words echoing through the palace halls. Without context, this statement doesn't carry much weight, so let's reflect on what led to this moment.

God's people were living in chaos. Originally, there were 12 tribes of Israel, made up of Jacob's sons and grandsons; however, they split in 930 BC. Ten tribes formed the independent Kingdom of Israel in the north: Asher, Dan, Ephraim, Gad, Issachar, Manasseh, Naphtali, Reuben, Simeon, and Zebulon, while Judah and

Benjamin formed the Kingdom of Judah in the south. Both kingdoms had many kings. Some were good, but most were unquestionably bad.

Josiah became the sixteenth king of Judah and reigned for thirty-one years. He is described as a righteous king who

"Did what was right in the eyes of the Lord and followed completely the ways of his father David, not turning aside to the right or the left." (2 Kings 22:2 NIV)

He is also mentioned in Jesus' genealogy. Quite impressive.

"God supports and heals: that's the Hebrew meaning of the name Josiah. For King Josiah, it's a perfect description. He was only eight years old when his father, Amon, was assassinated, and he ascended to the throne of Judah. While other young boys fished, skipped stones on the lake, and chased little girls, Josiah ruled the nation. It seemed like an impossible feat—a*n eight-year-old king?* However, he quickly became a royal powerhouse:

- At age sixteen, Josiah sought the Lord.
- When he was twenty, he began purging Judah of idolatry—destroying the altars of Baal, grinding up metal images, and executing idolatrous priests.

- At twenty-six, King Josiah began repairing the temple under the supervision of Hilkiah, the high priest who found the Book of the Law (the five books of Moses).

EXCITING DISCOVERY

During the temple repairs, a crew of workers discovered a scroll. It was an ancient scroll that appeared significant. They carefully removed the debris covering their fragile find. As they lifted the scroll, dust swirled from the rolled parchment, and they realized the significance of their discovery. Unsure of what they had uncovered, they brought it to Hilkiah, the priest, who examined it slowly and cautiously. It seemed incredible. Could it really be? So much time had passed.

The High Priest rushed to inform King Josiah of the discovery. When Josiah heard the news, he tore his clothes in anger (this was how people of that day expressed deep emotion). How could his father and grandfather have been so callous? They had shamelessly ridiculed and recklessly ignored the Law of Moses.

His grandfather, Manasseh, was the most wicked of them all. During his ungodly reign, the Word of God was nearly destroyed. The Passover Feast, which had been celebrated 900 years earlier, had not been observed since the days of Hezekiah, over sixty years before. They were as wicked as could be! But now Hilkiah stood before King Josiah, scroll in hand, and the king spoke:

"Go, inquire of the Lord for me,
for the people and for all of Judah,
concerning the words of this book
that has been found . . ."
(2 Kings 22:13 NKJV)

Hilkiah knew exactly where he'd go for that inquiry.

MEET HULDAH

Meanwhile, in the Second District of Jerusalem—the university district—shadows had grown long. The female students had already left the classroom, and Huldah was ready to end her day. She was a teacher of God's Law to women at a school she had founded. There, she shared her insights about God as they related to Jewish women, mothers, and daughters. She was married to Shallum, who was the keeper of the royal wardrobe.

She was cherished.

She was respected.

"Weasel or mole." That's the Hebrew meaning of the name *Huldah*. It's not exactly a flattering comparison for a woman, is it? Or for anyone, really. But when it comes to our Huldah, it's actually a compliment. How so? She was known for uncovering the truth of God's word. She dedicated herself to knowing the truth and sharing it with others. Again—that's quite a compliment. Huldah was not only a teacher of women but also God's prophetic voice to the king and the nation.

She's one of the few women in the Old Testament recognized as a prophet and is rarely discussed. It's possible to attend Sunday school and never hear her name. Let's face it, the name Huldah isn't popular in baby name books, unlike Abigail, Rachel, Rebecca, or even Miriam. It wasn't until 1900 that it reached its height in popularity, with only twenty-three girls named Huldah that year! It seems fitting: Huldah was a woman in a man's world.

She wasn't the only prophet during this time; she had several notable contemporaries, each of whom wrote books in the Bible:

- Nahum, God's messenger, proclaimed the fall of Nineveh and the total defeat of Assyria.
- Zephaniah warned Israel and the surrounding nations that the Day of the Lord was approaching. (He was intense.)
- And of course, there was Jeremiah, who proclaimed God's judgment on the people of his time for their wickedness. (Interesting fact: Some believe that Huldah was his aunt.)

Although Huldah doesn't have a book named after her—like many other Old Testament prophets—she's the one whom High Priest Hilkiah consulted regarding the king's inquiry.

"So Hilkiah the priest, Ahikam, Achbor, Shaphan, and Asaiah went to Huldah, the prophetess . . . and they spoke to her." (2 Kings 22:14 NKJV)

This temporal delegation speaks highly of Huldah. Her life has unquestionably earned the respect of both female and male authorities, not to mention the temporal and national power embodied in King Josiah.

This is a wonderful place for us to remember that it's not our education, experience, title, or gender that qualifies us to serve in God's Kingdom. Instead, it's our desire to serve and obey Him. When we walk in His will today, we establish a great pattern for walking in His will tomorrow.

Our responsibility is simply to align ourselves with God's call. That's our part—nothing more, nothing less. When we embrace our calling, there's no greater honor or higher prestige than this. It's an extraordinary place for our lives to reside. It's where Huldah lived, and God used her—an unexpected source—to deliver His message to the King.

"Then she said to them, 'Thus says the LORD God of Israel, tell the man who sent you to Me.' " (2 Kings 22:15 NKJV)

If there were any questions about where Huldah obtained her authority, she addressed them immediately.

When she spoke the words, "Thus says the LORD God of Israel," her source was unmistakable. She drew her authority from those four words:

"Thus

says

the

LORD."

It was recognizable because it was the language of the prophets. They served as His mouthpiece. When a prophet spoke, the crowd would hear His voice. Huldah directly responded to the King's inquiry on behalf of God. She used this language three times during her statement in verses 15 to 20. In verse 19, she said, "declares the Lord."

Therefore, when she spoke, she had no need to qualify or justify her words simply because she was a woman. She didn't have to fight for her right to be recognized as a prophet or to be heard. There was no need for her to explain herself. She knew who she was and who God had called her to be; therefore, she boldly fulfilled her office.

WHAT ABOUT YOU?

Do you struggle to accept who He has made you to be? Who He has called you to be? Perhaps you have a past—we all have a past—but we're talking about the past of all pasts! Now, God has called you to ministry, and the thoughts that keep you up at night are, "What will the people who *really* know me say?"

Or maybe you're like Huldah, a woman in what appears to be a man's world. You deserve that promotion, yet you're often overlooked. God has called you to preach, but due to traditional gender roles, you've faced many roadblocks, and you feel discouraged. Maybe it has even led to thoughts of quitting or simply giving up.

During those times, remember this:

You.

Are.

Not.

Alone.

Even Jesus faced this type of discouragement. In fact, fasten up—we're going jump ahead, way ahead in time, to one of those occasions.

JESUS STANDS OUT

In Mark 6, Jesus had been performing incredible acts. It's now well into the second year of His earthly ministry. Lives had been transformed, and the Kingdom was growing. Naturally, He wanted to advance that Kingdom in His hometown among His people. There's just something special about the place where we grow up.

On the Sabbath, Jesus taught in the synagogue. It felt natural as if He had been doing this since He was twelve. Do you remember how the teachers of the Law were amazed by His teachings in the temple in Jerusalem? Not much had changed. How can we tell? By the reactions of the listeners. Typically, when Jesus taught, their jaws would drop. A day like this in the synagogue was rare and distinctly different from the mundane mediocrity they had become accustomed to.

It was different.

So new.

So attractive.

Usually. But not today.

In verse 2, the people were astonished and questioned what they were hearing. Unfortunately, by verse 3, something changed. Their astonishment turned into skepticism and, ultimately, offense.

"Isn't this Mary's son?"

"Didn't he come from *here?"*

"Hey, we changed His diapers!"

Sadly, while others questioned whether anything good could come from Nazareth, they had already made up their minds: It couldn't. The result is found in verse five: Jesus was unable to do mighty works in His hometown, and He marveled because of their unbelief. In their minds, Jesus was just a hometown boy who forgot where He came from. That's all.

HULDAH'S IDENTITY

Once again, Huldah recognized the source of her authority: God Himself. She spoke on His behalf, fulfilling her purpose. If God has called you to preach, to be a missionary, or to sing, remember that your authority comes from Him. He qualifies your calling and equips those He calls for ministry. Ignore the naysayers, and don't let your past haunt you. Walk boldly with Him and remember who you are. Huldah did!

"Thus says the LORD: Behold, I will bring calamity on this place and on its inhabitants—all the words of the book which the king of Judah has read—because they have forsaken Me and burned incense to other gods, that they might provoke me to anger with all the works of their hands. Therefore My wrath shall be aroused against this place and shall not be quenched." (2 Kings 22:16-17 NKJV)

So, what was the message Huldah sent to the king?
(If this were a movie, we'd cue ominous music here.)
CALAMITY.
Consider that . . .
Misery.
Disaster.
Adversity.
Great Misfortune.
Grievous Affliction.
Yikes!

WARNING

That's the Word of the LORD which Huldah spoke to the King.

It was a dire prophecy that concluded with God saying, "His wrath . . . shall not be quenched."

Why such a strong judgment? Huldah revealed the answer in her prophecy: "Because *they have forsaken Me* (God)."

There's a genuine danger when we choose to ignore God's instructions and His word. This dreadful prophecy stemmed from more than fifty-seven years of disregarding God and what He said. Remember the earlier mention of Josiah's grandfather Manasseh? He was the most ungodly king of all, and he nearly obliterated the Word of God. That's where the neglect started.

During his reign, Grandfather Manasseh revoked the reforms that his great-grandfather Hezekiah, *one of the good kings*, had made. Sadly, he ruled nearly twice as long, the longest of any Davidic king, and was known for his wickedness.

What could've been so bad? Here's a brief list:

- He reconstructed the high places and altars to Baal.
- He placed an image of Asherah in the temple.
- He worshipped other gods.
- He engaged in child sacrifice and spirit divination.

Manasseh was an extremely evil king who plunged Judah into darkness for fifty-five years. He desecrated the temple so severely that prophets declared him worse than the Amorites whom the Israelites had originally expelled from the land.

Fortunately, Manasseh repented near the end of his life. However, although his sins were forgiven, the consequences of those sins could not be avoided. Amon, Josiah's father, was one such consequence.

INFLUENCE

Parents have a profound influence on their children, and Amon was no exception. Influenced by Manasseh for many years, he continued his father's wicked practices, and the darkness only intensified. His reign was brief—just two years—yet he was such an evil king that his royal officials assassinated him, paving the way for Josiah to become king.

Remember, Josiah was only eight years of age when he began his rule, so the influence of his father and grandfather hadn't been able to pollute the tender heart of the young king.

Neglecting God and His word has significant consequences. We cannot avoid the outcomes of our choices. It's the law of consequence: We reap what we sow.

This would be a great place to pause for personal introspection, understanding that what we choose to do (or not do) will affect not only us but also others. Judah would pay a high price for the sins of her Kings.

"But as for the king of Judah,
who sent you to inquire of the LORD, in
this manner you shall speak to him. . . ."
(2 Kings 22:18 NKJV)

Have you ever noticed how powerful the word *but* is? It doesn't seem significant—some might say it's puny, *but* it has the power to change the entire story. (Do you see what I did there?) It's a coordinating conjunction that connects ideas. It's used to link something that contrasts with what has already been mentioned. Look at the beginning of this paragraph again:

But is powerful, *but* puny; it's puny *but* has potential. Get it?

Huldah had just pronounced the consequences of neglecting not only the words of God but God Himself. Those consequences were CALAMITY. Due to this neglect, there would be suffering, misery, and disaster. It was a dire prophecy that would be disheartening for anyone receiving the news. The outcome would bring dread, fear, and anxiety. All hope would vanish. That was until she said, "But for the king of Judah . . . speak to him in this manner . . ."

Can you sense the change in Huldah's tone? She had previously spoken God's judgments in a very stern, scolding manner, but now we see a shift to the reward of obedience.

Obedience is always rewarded.

WAY BACK WHEN

From the beginning of time, the hallmark of true love has been obedience. Man's purpose was to engage in a beautiful and complete relationship with his Creator. However, it's essential to recognize that a forced relationship isn't a relationship at all. Therefore, there needed to be a way for man to reciprocate that love, which would be through obedience. *"Don't eat from the tree . . ."* yet they did, and the relationship was broken.

Again, the mark of true love has always been and will always be absolute obedience—total, unconditional obedience to His voice. For a complete relationship, there must be total obedience, and that obedience is always rewarded by His presence. Remember the words of John:

"When we obey God, we are sure we know Him. But if we claim to know Him and don't obey Him the truth isn't in our hearts. We truly love God only when we obey Him as we should, and then we know we belong to Him. If we say we are His, we must follow the example of Christ." (1 John 2:3-6: CEV)

Simply put, our lives will reveal whether or not we love Him through our obedience to His Word. Josiah will soon be rewarded for his obedience.

How?

Huldah continued:

"Thus says the LORD God of Israel: 'Concerning the words which you have heard—because you heart was tender, and you humbled yourself before the LORD when you heard what I spoke against this place and against its

inhabitants . . . you tore your clothes and wept before Me, I also have heard you,' says the LORD. Surely, therefore, I will gather you to your fathers, and you shall be gathered to your grave in peace, and your eyes shall not see all the calamity which I will bring on this place." (2 Kings 22:18-20 NKJV)

"Your eyes shall not see all the calamity. You will die in peace." This is the message God conveyed through Huldah to King Josiah. After delivering such a grave prophecy regarding the neglect of His words, we now hear of the reward. God will show Josiah favor during his reign over Judah.

The consequences of neglect were unavoidable, but they would not occur under Josiah's rule. Again—obedience is always rewarded. History will depict him as a righteous king who

"walked in all the ways of his father David; he did not turn aside to the right hand or to the left." (2 Kings 22:2; 2 Chronicles 34:2 NKJV)

ACTION

After receiving the prophecy from Huldah, Josiah removed all the idolatrous items in the Kingdom of Judah. He renewed the covenant between God and His people and concluded the reforms with a grand celebration of the Feast of Unleavened Bread and the

Passover. (Do you remember they hadn't celebrated the Passover since Hezekiah's reign nearly sixty years prior?!)

It must have been quite a celebration, because we're told,

"Such a Passover surely had never been held since the days of the judges who judged Israel, nor in all the days of the kings of Israel and the kings of Judah." (2 Kings 23:22 NKJV)

In a time of darkness, there was a light: a prophet named Huldah, known for uncovering the truth of God's word. A woman in a man's world, sought by the king for answers. She didn't shy away from that task; instead, she stood firm in who God called her to be and delivered His messages. And because she did, things changed.

The true test of a prophet is whether the prophecy is fulfilled, and Huldah's proved to be accurate. King Josiah reigned for another thirteen years, totaling thirty-one years. He didn't have to witness the destruction of Jerusalem, as God spared him from the calamity that occurred at the end of his son Zedekiah's eleven-year reign. Huldah was also spared from witnessing the destruction.

God is in the business of using people—both women and men—in powerful ways to proclaim His word. If we allow this, it could lead to monumental change. God used Huldah in this manner, and He can use you, too.

Huldah was definitely a hit.

Just ask Josiah.

GOING DEEPER

- Have you ever felt that the Lord was calling you to a specific task, but questioned your ability to do it? What caused your doubts? How did you overcome them?
- As you reflect on your walk with Jesus, do you feel a sense of closeness to Him through His word? How much time do you dedicate to reading His word?
- We discussed the law of consequences—reaping what we sow. Think about a time when you followed God's voice in your life (maybe it was difficult) and how you felt God's blessing through your obedience. Or share an experience when you didn't obey and what the outcome was.
- Huldah's life influenced King Josiah and many others. Who has positively impacted your life? How can you similarly influence others?

HULDAH WAS A WOMAN IN A MAN'S WORLD.

OBEDIENCE IS ALWAYS REWARDED.

THERE'S A REAL DANGER WHEN WE CHOOSE TO NEGLECT GOD'S WORD.

ONE-HIT WONDER: NORMAN GREENBAUM

Let's go back to 1969. Can you recall a song by Norman Greenbaum written with a Christian theme? I'm guessing it would sound familiar to you if you heard it.

It's called "Spirit in the Sky." Go ahead and find it on YouTube and hum along.

Unfortunately, that's all that Norman Greenbaum is known for. He was a one-hit wonder.

CHAPTER SIXTEEN

(Judges 11-12)

Jephthah's Rash Promise

Be very cautious about the promises you make.
Think it over carefully before committing to a vow.

Allow me to introduce you to Jephthah:

"Jephthah the Gileadite was a mighty warrior. His father was Gilead; his mother was a prostitute. Gilead's wife also bore him sons, and when they were grown up, they drove Jephthah away. " 'You are not going to get any inheritance in our family,' they said, 'because you are the son of another woman.' "
(Judges 11:1-2 NIV)

Jephthah's brothers ostracized him. They cast him out. They chased him away from his family and his hometown.

He

wasn't

wanted.

Jephthah was born because of his father's relationship with a prostitute. In Jephthah's society and time, being born out of wedlock carried a severe social stigma.

Wherever he went, he was the target of jokes, teased, and taunted. He wasn't even accepted by his own family—he was an outcast.

But guess what! God loves to use those who feel like outsiders!

There's an important fact to understand about Jephthah as we start his story. Despite being the son of a prostitute and leading a street gang—and despite making seven quick, poorly thought-out vows before God—his name is one of only sixteen mentioned in the Hall of Faith in Hebrews 11.

This shows us that regardless our past—if God used Jephthah, He can use us! God *often* uses the unexpected as His instruments to accomplish His purposes:

- The rod of Moses
- A boat built by Noah and his sons
- David's slingshot
- A manger

And God has a history of using the most unexpected, unqualified people.

Moses stuttered.

David's armor didn't fit.

Jacob was a liar.

Solomon was too rich.

Abraham was too old.

David was too young. Naomi was a widow.

Martha was a worrywart.

Jonah ran from God. Gideon and Thomas both doubted God.

Jeremiah was depressed.

Elijah was burned out.

Timothy had ulcers.

Peter was afraid of death.

And of course—Lazarus *was* dead.

Then . . . there's Jephthah. The son of a prostitute.

Throughout the Bible, we encounter individuals who appear unlikely and unqualified to be used. Jephthah definitely fits this description. And this should encourage us! We can say, "Lord, in spite of my failures, I'm moving forward with You. I want You to use me to bring glory to Your name."

Are you familiar with the song, "Use Me" by Ron Kenoly?

"If you can use anything, Lord, You can use me . . ." (*Search for it on YouTube and give it a good listen.*)

There's so much truth in this song. If He truly *can* use anything—He used a donkey to speak, a fish to catch a prophet—then He can definitely use me! Okay, let's go back to Jephthah.

JEPHTHAH'S STORY

His brothers kicked him out of the family. Let's look at Scripture and see what happens next:

"So Jephthah fled from his brothers and settled in the land of Tob, where a gang of scoundrels gathered around him and followed him." (Judges 11:3 NIV)

Jephthah went to Tob—an area known for its killers, raiders, and thieves. I can see him and his men now: the Tob Mob.

They were probably dressed in black leather jackets and riding loud, unmuffled donkeys from party to party. Jephthah was the leader, so maybe he had a souped-up chariot and a two-humped camel. Let's keep reading:

"Some time later, when the Ammonites were fighting against Israel, the elders of Gilead went to get Jephthah from the land of Tob. " 'Come,' they said, 'be our commander, so we can fight the Ammonites.' " (Judges 11:4-6 NIV)

What's happening here?

The Israelites were threatened by the Ammonites, so they went to the toughest guy they knew—Jephthah—and begged him to fight for them.

This was definitely something Jephthah could do.

It would be like asking legendary basketball star Michael Jordan to play on the church team or asking Tiger Woods to coach the high school golf team.

How did Jephthah respond? Let's move on to the next verse:

"Jephthah said to them,
'Didn't you hate me and drive me from my
father's house? Why do you come to me
now, when you're in trouble?' "
(Judges 4:7 NIV)

Good question! Let's look at their answer.

"The elders of Gilead said
to him, 'Nevertheless, we are turning
to you now; come with us to fight
the Ammonites, and you will be head
over all of us who live in Gilead.' "
(Judges 11:8 NIV)

So, this tough guy from Tob was the leader of the entire Israelite army. While he hung out in the wilderness of Tob, something was happening to Jephthah.

He was learning that if God was involved in something, it couldn't fail.

How do we know this? It's because of the statement he makes in the next verse:

"Jephthah said to the elders of Gilead, 'If you bring me home again to fight against the Ammonites, and the Lord gives them over to me, I will be your head.' " (Judges 11:9 ESV)

Jephthah knew he was tough, but he also understood that God was supreme. He was wise enough to see that his success depended on God's help. He thought, "*If God is in this, I'll be victorious.*"

This makes me think of the letter to the church in Philadelphia found in the book of Revelation.

"I have opened a door for you that no man can close." (Revelation 3:8 NLT)

Let that inspire you! If God opens a door, no one can shut it. It might seem like your closed door will never reopen, but if God intends for you to go through, He'll open it. The closure is only temporary.

Remember Joseph from the Old Testament? He spent years in jail for a crime he didn't commit. It seemed like God's dreams for him were only dreams. But when God opened the door, Joseph became second in command to Pharaoh—at that time, the most powerful person in the world. God always keeps His promises.

Jephthah and the elders traveled from Tob back to Gilead. They organized a large assembly, standing in solemnity before the Lord as Jephthah took the oath of office before Him.

Jephthah was willing to walk through the open door. He was intelligent, and before fighting, he tried to achieve peace through diplomatic talks.

Judges 11:12-28 detail his diplomatic efforts to settle the conflict with the Ammonites.

HE KNEW THE RIGHT STUFF

In recounting the history of the disputed land, Jephthah traveled back 300 years in Israel's past. He revealed in precise detail his knowledge of Numbers 20, which was almost a direct quote.

It's important to understand our spiritual history. God has given you a spiritual history through His Word. In the Old Testament, the Jews were instructed to put a pillar in a specific place. They were told that when their children asked what that rock meant, they should tell them the story of how they were led out of Egypt.

How well do you know the Bible?

Do you read it consistently?

Do you study it?

I heard of a recent poll showing that the majority of churchgoers only read the Bible when it's displayed on the screen during the pastor's sermon on Sunday mornings. It's going to take more than this to become all God desires of us.

Jephthah recounted the story using Scripture with complete accuracy. He quoted his Bible and trusted it to be historically accurate.

I love this! We're now seeing pastors denying the existence of heaven and hell. Some pastors are good people, but they're misled. One way to identify false teachings is to check the source. Is the teacher relying on a popular book or the Bible?

Are you implying that using a book with godly principles in teaching is wrong? Not at all—if those principles are supported by Scripture. We need to know God's Word so well that when we hear or read false teaching, we instantly identify it as false.

There isn't enough space in this chapter to discuss all the movies with misleading messages, but I'd like to mention one aimed at children: *Trolls,* released in 2016 by DreamWorks.

The film's theme song, Justin Timberlake's "Can't Stop the Feeling," is an upbeat tune. The animated version is available on YouTube. Before the song starts, you'll hear a few seconds of dialogue. What is this dialogue that has been played more than *600 million* times?

King Gristle Sr.: "Do you really think I can be happy?"
Poppy: "Of course! It's inside you! It's inside of all of us! And I don't *think* it; I *feel* it!

Nowadays, pilgrimages to find truth, beauty and goodness don't require a plane ticket. Just a mirror. The world's soundtrack sounds like this:

"Follow your heart."

"Be true to yourself."

"Find yourself."

"Love yourself."

"Express yourself."

"Believe in yourself."

The Bible doesn't talk this way. In fact, it's striking to me just how *differently* Scripture employs the *same* words.

World: "Follow your heart."
Jesus: "Follow me." (Matthew 10:38)

World: "Love yourself."
Jesus: "Love the Lord your God [and] love your neighbor." (Mark 12:30–31)

World: "Discover yourself."
Jesus: "Deny yourself." (Luke 9:23)

World: "Believe in yourself."
Jesus: "Believe in me." (John 6:35)

The world tells us that SELF needs to be front and center. Jephthah knew better. He realized that without God, his efforts would be in vain.

It's crucial for Christians to use discernment regarding popular teachings and let God's Word judge men's words. Here are some Scripture references that will encourage you to stand firm against false teachings:

Romans 16:17

Acts 17:11

Colossians 2:8

1 Peter 5:8

2 Timothy 4:3-4

1 John 4:1

Jephthah knew God's Word. Unfortunately, many people in the church claim to be Christians but don't really know the Bible. Many Christians have never made the effort to read the Old Testament, and some have never read the Bible in its entirety.

We need to examine ourselves, and if we fall short in this area, we should commit to God to read the Bible for at least five minutes every day and pray He will give us a hunger for more.

Jephthah trusts in God's Word. He believes that when it delivers a message, God has spoken, and its statements and promises are reliable.

JEPHTHAH IS A MAN WHO TOOK HIS FAITH SERIOUSLY

He knew God's word! Yes, he had taken a few wrong turns, but now he has taken an oath before the Lord to become a godly leader. His knowledge of Scripture is now permeating his life.

One of the Holy Spirit's job descriptions is to remind us of God's Word. But He can't remind us if we don't know it. Jephthah tried three times to use diplomacy with the Ammonites, but they refused to listen. They were ready to fight.

So Jephthah organized his troops. He's experiencing God's anointing. But OOPS! Instead of simply proceeding in faith, Jephthah made a vow to the Lord. All these centuries later, this is the main reason he's remembered.

What was his vow? Let's continue with Scripture in Judges 11:30-31:

"And Jephthah made a vow to the Lord: 'If you give the Ammonites into my hands, whatever comes out of the door of my house to meet me when I return in triumph from the Ammonites will be the Lord's, and I will sacrifice it as a burnt offering." (Judges 11:30-31 NIV)

He was obviously thinking it would be a bull, a sheep, or a goat.

Until his vow, he acted as a sincere worshiper of Jehovah.

- He forgave those who had mistreated him.
- He prayed for the blessing of the Lord.
- He received a special anointing of the Spirit.
- He wasn't eager to shed blood. He tried to resolve the land dispute by diplomacy.

But in a moment of desperation, he went one step further.

He made a rash vow to the Lord.

HEADED HOME

Let's return from battle with Jephthah and go home with him through Scripture:

"When Jephthah returned home his daughter—his only child—ran out to meet him, playing on a tambourine and dancing for joy. When he saw her, he tore his clothes in anguish." (Judges 11:34-35 TLB)

It seems he didn't expect his daughter to be home. Let's read the rest of verse 35:

" 'Alas, my daughter!' he cried out. 'You have brought me to the dust. For I have made a vow to the Lord and I cannot take it back.' " (Judges 11:35 TLB)

What did she feel about her father's anguish and the sudden realization of her own destiny? Her response was heroic. Let's take a closer look at Judges 11:36.

"And she said, 'Father, you must do whatever you promised the Lord, for he has given you a great victory over your enemies, the Ammonites.' "
(Judges 11:36 TLB)

I hear her saying, "Dad, you're a man of integrity. Don't back down now." Parents, your children want you to be godly. They *need* you to be moms and dads of integrity.

His daughter's reaction carried no resentful or rebellious tones.

She shed no tears nor shook with despair—after her father, with a crushed heart, spoke of his vow.

There was quiet acceptance of the tragic fact that she was going to be the sacrifice her father had promised.

Currently, we do not know her name. She is only recognized as "Jephthah's daughter." While she may not have had the gifts and talents of some other women in the Bible, she'll always be remembered for her role as a willing sacrifice in biblical history.

I'm sure at this point, all kinds of thoughts were racing through Jephthah's mind: *Nobody heard me make that vow. It was just between God and me. Maybe I don't need to keep it.*

OR *Lord, You know I was under a lot of stress when I made that vow. I can't keep this promise.*

How easy it would've been for Jephthah to rationalize his way out of it. But watch what happens with his daughter:

"'But first let me go up into the hills and roam with my girlfriends for two months, weeping because I'll never marry.'
"'Yes,' he said. 'Go.'
"And so she did, bewailing her fate with her friends for two months.
"Then she returned to her father, who did as he had vowed.
So she was never married."
(Judges 11:37-38 TLB)

So Jephthah's daughter and her girlfriends did what all women do when their dreams are dashed—they went on a two-month road trip and ate non-stop ice cream straight from the cartons for ten weeks.

SERIOUSLY?

Most Bible scholars conclude that Jephthah didn't kill his daughter; instead, he sacrificed her by promising she would never marry, which at the time was almost the same as being dead.

She would never have children, and Jephthah's family would be disconnected from Israel, causing his inheritance to pass to someone else. Many Bible scholars believe he didn't kill her because he was a godly man, and human sacrifice was not only detestable to God but also strictly forbidden.

Keep in mind that God honored Jephthah by including him in the Faith Hero Hall of Fame in Hebrews 11.

Do you believe God would honor a man who defied His command against human sacrifice by including him in the Hall of Faith?

I don't think so.

And the book of Judges never condemns Jephthah for his actions.

If he had killed her, I believe Scripture would have condemned him.

But Jephthah's vow was a foolish vow, because:

- It required someone else to sacrifice more than himself.
- It was a foolish vow because:
- It was illegal by the laws of God and man.
- It was a self-serving vow with an "if" clause.

Let's take another look at the Scripture we just read:

"Then she returned to her father,
who did as he had vowed.
So she was never married."
(Judges 11:39 TLB)

The phrase "so she was never married" alludes to the fact that this was the sacrifice. The key point is that God wants us to take our vows seriously.

"I will fulfill my vows to the Lord in the presence of all his people." (Psalm 116:18 NIV)

If we say we'll do something, we need to do it.

God wants us to see that Jephthah was willing to sacrifice his only child for Him. Can you even imagine? Who in the world would do such a thing?

And yet we can recall another Scripture:

"For God so loved the world, that he gave his only begotten Son, that whosoever believeth in him should not perish, but have everlasting life." (John 3:16 KJV)

We learn some important truths from Jephthah's story:

TRUTH #1: NO MATTER YOUR PAST, GOD STILL DREAMS BIG FOR YOU!

(Check out Ephesians 3:20) Let God forgive your past and move forward. He wants to use you!

TRUTH #2: GOD DESIRES FOR US TO HANDLE CONFLICT PEACEFULLY.

Is there conflict in your life? Are you having an argument with someone? Resolve it! Do you need to forgive someone? Do it!

TRUTH #3: KNOW GOD'S WORD.

God has given you a spiritual heritage, and it's found in the Bible.

Read it! Study it! It's essential for becoming everything He's calling you to be.

TRUTH #4: GOD DESIRES YOUR VOWS.

Let's go to Scripture:

"When you make a vow to God do not delay to fulfill it. He has no pleasure in fools; fulfill your vow." (Ecclesiastes 5:4 NIV)

According to Scripture, God considers us fools if we make vows and fail to keep them!

He wants you to make promises to Him.

But ask His help.

Allow Him to guide you to make wise vows.

Then seek His discipline to fulfill them.

TRUTH #5: GOD WILL ALWAYS HONOR SACRIFICIAL OBEDIENCE.

- Hannah: Gave her son Samuel.
- The poor widow in Mark 12:41-44 who gave her last two cents. (See chapter 12)

Could He be calling you to make a sacrificial commitment? God doesn't want us to sweeten the pot or negotiate with Him. He wants our trust. And the bottom line is that we *can* trust Him. We don't need to play games with God. He is faithful.

GOING DEEPER

- What have you learned from Jephthah's story?
- Do you find yourself sometimes using bargaining words with God, trying to make a deal with Him?
- Go to YouTube and listen to Ron Kenoly's "Use Me." Ask God to reveal something He wants to do through you as you listen to the music.
- Listen to Babbie Mason's song "Trust His Heart." You can find it on YouTube. Ask God to deepen your faith in Him.

Jephthah has faith in God's word.

He was learning that if God was involved in something, it couldn't fail.

God loves to use those who feel like outsiders.

ONE-HIT WONDER: DAVE KAPELL

Who could guess that a sneeze could lead to a money-maker? Dave Kapell was a musician with terrible allergies. In 1993, he was struggling with writer's block and sneezed over some cut-up song lyrics he'd written. The little papers scattered across his desk.

He realized he could easily create wacky sentences and fun slogans with the messed-up slips of paper. He put magnets on his words and attached them to a baking tray so he could easily move them around and create sentences without much effort.

In 1995, Dave began selling his magnetic poetry kits in bookstores and gift shops. Years later, he's still using this idea with some different variations. He's a one-hit poetry wonder.

CHAPTER SEVENTEEN

(Judges 10:1-2)

Case Dismissed

This incredible account with Tola will take you on a much deeper journey when you go beyond what's presented at face value, explore behind the scenes, and experience its transformative power.

After studying something for a while, we can sometimes find a hidden message beneath the surface. Take for instance these well-known logos. At first glance, we simply see the title and the logo. But when we look a bit deeper, we see more meaning deeper within.

TOSTITOS

Who doesn't like to munch on crispy Tostito chips? Do a google search for the logo. The two Ts are designed to be people dipping the yellow chip into the red bowl of salsa just above the "i." Clever, huh!

KISSES

Do you like Hershey's Kisses? Look up their logo. We can easily see the two obvious silver kisses in the logo. But by studying it more carefully, you'll discover there's actually a third kiss. It's between the K and the I.

AMAZON

I'm guessing you've probably used Amazon. The company's current logo debuted in 2000 and contains a message that reflects its wide range of business interests. When you see their logo, notice the arrow swoops from the first "a" to the "z" to demonstrate that the company sells everything from A to Z.

YUMMY BURGERS

Wendy's is a favorite for lots of people. But Dave Thomas, the founder, wanted the design in the logo to reflect family. If you'll look closely, you'll notice Wendy's collar spells out MOM. collar spells out MOM in black. the red-haired daughter of Dave Thomas, the founder of Wendy's, wanted the design in the logo to reflect family.

We wouldn't have noticed the deeper message in these logos without taking a closer look. And oftentimes it works the same way in Scripture. By studying—and gazing deeper—there are times we get much more than we expected. That's where we're headed with a seemingly obscure passage from the Old Testament book of Judges.

"After Abimelech's death, the next judge of Israel was Tola (son of Puah and grandson of Dodo).

"He was from the tribe of Issachar but lived in the city of Shamir in the hill country of Ephraim.

"He was Israel's judge for twenty-three years. When he died, he was buried in Shamir" (Judges 10:1-2 TLB)

So, Tola was a judge in Israel. He defended people. And he was a righteous judge. Let's look at this same passage from the New International Version:

"After the time of Abimelek,
a man of Issachar named Tola son of
Puah, the son of Dodo, rose to save Israel.
"He lived in Shamir, in the hill country of
Ephraim. He led Israel twenty-three years;
then he died, and was buried in Shamir."
(Judges 10:1-2 NIV)

Tola's dad's name, *Puah,* means "**splendid.**"

His grandfather's name, *Dodo,* means "**beloved one.**"

But Tola's name meant neither "splendid" nor "beloved."

The name Tola means **"WORM."**

Can you imagine being named "worm"?

"Hi, I'm Susie."

"Hi, Susie. I'm . . . *worm.*"

Tola's name meant "WORM!" He was a man of Issachar who lived in Ephraim. In other words, he wasn't living among his own people. He had moved away.

People in the moving biz have lots of stories to tell. Here's one that caught my attention:

"A customer asked me whether his iguana could travel in the front seat of the truck during the move. 'She's small and won't take much room.'

"I'm not very familiar with lizards, and in my vivid imagination, an iguana kind of resembles a small crocodile. So, while frantically searching for images of iguanas online to buy some time, I asked the guy what size of cage the iguana would be traveling in.

"'Cage? No. She doesn't have a cage. She'll ride in the passenger's seat. She's very calm and quiet. I can't hurt an innocent animal by putting it in a cage. The poor thing is already so stressed because of this move!'

"Seriously? It took a lot of explaining to make it clear that no driver would volunteer to travel with an uncaged iguana in the front seat."

Tola probably didn't have to share his chariot with an iguana, but he had definitely made a move. He wasn't living among his own people.

FAR AWAY

Maybe you know what it's like to live away from family. For many it's college. For me (Susie), it was after college. I moved from OKC to Conway, Arkansas to become a youth pastor.

I arrived on Saturday and hit the ground running: I taught the youth group on Sunday morning, and the next day, I left with the teens for camp.

I loved being a youth pastor.

And I loved my youth group.

But it was my first time to live away from home, and even though I was only six hours from my home in OKC, it was a bit tough living in another state.

I missed family.

I missed having close friends my own age.

And I can't help but wonder if Tola felt this way.

Did he miss his family? Why was he living away from them?

Scripture doesn't give us this information, so I did some research. He moved to Mt. Ephraim which was more in the heart of the country, and it was more convenient there for the people to come to him for judgment (for him to hear their problems and defend them).

We can think of Someone else who left His home.

His name is JESUS.

Not only did He leave His home in heaven—but according to John 1:11—He chose to live among people who didn't accept Him.

Let's take a look:

"Even in his own land and among his own people, the Jews, he was not accepted. Only a few would welcome and receive him." (John 1:11 TLB)

Of course, we know our Savior by the name JESUS. But He calls Himself by another name in the Old Testament:

**"But I am a worm, not a man,
scorned and despised by my own
people and by all mankind."
(Psalm 22:6 TLB)**

Why would Jesus say He's a worm?

Hang on—we'll get to that in a sec.

Right now, let's get back to the name TOLA.

The Hebrew word Tola looks like this:

איך ט ולה

And it's translated two ways in the Bible: *scarlet* and *worm*.

Let's Go Deeper

Why would the same word be used for both "scarlet" and "worm"?

Cuz in Bible days, when people needed scarlet cloth, they'd grind worms into a pasty, blood-red substance that would be used as a dye.

Did you know there's an actual Tola worm? Go ahead: Do a google search and find a photo of this worm.

Why would Jesus say that He's a worm? We'll get the answer by taking a closer look at the Tola worm. To reproduce—the tola worm will climb the trunk of a tree and fasten itself onto a limb.

Then the worm will lay the larva and cover the eggs with its body.

Although the eggs will hatch, the worm won't budge.

So, the larva begins to feed on the body of the one who has given them life. As the Tola gave its' life for the babies, its' blood would leave a scarlet mark on the tree. Please search for a photo of this. It's fascinating.

After the dead worm fell, the bloody spot left on the limb of the tree would dry after three days and become a white, flaky substance that would fall to the ground like snow. Again, find a photo of this. You'll be amazed at the parallel.

"Though your sins are like scarlet—
***tola*—they shall be as white as snow."**
(Isaiah 1:18 ESV)

The tola worm is also known as the "crimson worm."

Fastened to the tree of the Cross of Calvary, Jesus wouldn't budge until the work was finished. What work?

The work that would allow you and me to be "hatched"—to be born again. The Tola worm and its larva is biological.

What Jesus did is pure love.

The tola larva doesn't have a choice.

We do.

BUT JUST WHAT IF?

Let's imagine the tola larva *did* have a choice. Let's pretend that larva can think. Let's crawl inside a pretend mind of larva.

I hear the larva saying, "I know I'm supposed to eat off of the worm, but I'm tired of worm juice. I want some tacos. I'm crawling out from underneath this worm and heading to the Food Court!"

The sad ending is that the larva will immediately die once it's prematurely separated from the worm who gave it birth.

But some of us are like that.

We were born with a deadly disease called sin.

It's evil, and it lurks within all of us.

We'll die unless we get the cure, the remedy.

Jesus Christ says, "I will be the Remedy. I'll give My blood.

My life. Eat of Me. Drink of Me. I'm the cure.

I'll die so you won't have to."

It's hard for me to understand why people *don't* choose Christ, but by *not* choosing to attach ourselves to Him, we're choosing eternal death.

This Old Testament passage reads as though God is begging us to choose life!

"I call heaven and earth to witness against you that today I have set before you life or death . . . Oh, that you would choose life! (Deuteronomy 30:19 TLB)

Let's get back inside the pretend mind of the larva. I hear another one saying, "Thank you for giving me this nourishment. Thank you for giving me life. I'd never have life if you hadn't chosen to give yourself so I could live."

Now we understand why Jesus calls Himself a worm in Psalm 22:6.

Let's look at it again:

"But I am a worm, not a man, scorned and despised by my own people and by all mankind." (Psalm 22:6 TLB)

Huh?

He was speaking prophetically. He knew He would willingly give His life—like the tola worm—so we could live.

"Eat of My Body," He says in Mark 14:22.

"Drink of My blood. I give My life for you."

THIS is why we have communion.

Christ *willingly* gave His body and His blood—His very LIFE—so we can live! And not just live, but THRIVE!

Let's go back to the Scripture we began with:

"After Abimelech's death, the next judge of Israel was Tola. . . ." (Judges 10:1 TLB)

Let's remember that Tola was a righteous judge. Well, by His blood, Jesus is a righteous Judge times a bazillion. He's a righteous Judge who *defends* us.

Revelation 12:10 tells us that Satan accuses us day and night, going before the Throne of the Father saying, "Look at him. Look at her. They've blown it here. They've messed up there."

But the Bible says the accuser was overcome by the blood of the Lamb. Jesus defeated Satan! When Jesus willingly gave His life on the Cross for you and for me—He defeated Satan the accuser!

"If any man sin, we have an advocate with the Father, Jesus Christ the righteous." (1 John 2:1 KJV)

This means that when we sin, if we'll seek Christ's forgiveness (although Satan will be at the throne of God pointing out our failures and shortcomings), we have a Defender—the Tola—the scarlet Worm, Jesus—who says, "Father, she has eaten of My body. He has tasted of My blood. They are clean!"

God hears the accusations of the accuser (the prosecuting attorney)—but thankfully He also hears the defense of His Son! And Father God hits the gavel in the courtroom of heaven and says, "Case dismissed for lack of evidence!"

And celebration breaks forth.

TOLA! **The Worm.**

TOLA! **The Defender.**

TOLA! **The One who died so you can live.**

TOLA! **Christ who gives His *everything* to you *right now!***

Maybe you need a Defender. The accuser berates you. Hates you.

Your advocate, JC, loves you unconditionally.

Forgives you extravagantly.

Restores you completely.

When we are at the edge of damnation, Christ says, "You are no longer damned! Case dismissed!"

Oh, what powerful words.

Beautiful. Healing. Redemptive words.

Maybe you'd like to pray, "Jesus, I'm sorry for trying to find life on my own. I'm nothing more than dead larva without Your saving blood. So I'm asking You to forgive me. I want to LIVE. And I want to live for You!"

Perhaps you've already made this commitment . . . but you've never really thought about Christ calling Himself a worm and the reason behind it.

And now that you've seen a clear word picture of Him firmly attaching Himself to the Tree—the Cross—you just want to say an overwhelming "THANK YOU, Jesus!"

It's time for us to make a move: Either to seek His forgiveness and accept His life in us.

Or to come in gratitude and humility and say *thank You.*

As we close this chapter—and this book—will you us a favor? Watch the music video on YouTube: "Selah - There is a Fountain" and spend time talking with your heavenly Father.

There's an old hymn that churches don't sing much anymore.

THE OLD RUGGED CROSS

(by George Bennard)

"On a hill far away stood an old rugged Cross
the emblem of suff'ring and shame;
And I love that old Cross, where the dearest and best
for a world of lost sinners was slain.

(Chorus:)
So I'll cherish the old rugged Cross,
till my trophies at last I lay down.
I will cling to the old rugged Cross,
and exchange it someday for a crown."

O, the old rugged cross, so despised by the world
Has a wondrous attraction for me;
For the dear Lamb of God left His glory above
To bear it to dark Calvary.

GOING DEEPER

- **Identify a time when you defended someone. How did they respond?**
- **Share a time when someone defended you. How did it make you feel?**
- **When we think of the word *judge*, we tend to think of someone who pronounces us innocent or guilty. But a judge is also a defender. Does this change your view of Jesus in any way?**

Maybe you know what it's like to live away from family.

Tola was a righteous judge.

Fastened to the tree of the cross of Calvary, Jesus wouldn't budge until the work was finished.

ABOUT THE AUTHORS

REV. SUSIE SHELLENBERGER holds a Doctorate of Divinity and is the senior pastor of Lake View Park Church of the Nazarene in Oklahoma City, OK. She's a former youth pastor, high school teacher, magazine editor, radio show host, and evangelist. She has led approximately 6,000 people on various international mission trips and has seen more than 15,000 commitments to Christ on these ventures. Susie is an OKC Thunder basketball fan and sometimes gives the invocation at home games. She's in demand as a national speaker in churches and at women's conferences and retreats. She has two dogs: Bentley Boy and Boone Doggie.

REV. BILLY HUDDLESTON is a fulltime evangelist who speaks 48 weeks each year. He delivers fast-paced messages laced with humor and Scriptural depth. Billy is also an accomplished vocalist with several CDs and has his own radio show. Billy is a high-energy communicator who loves leading people deeper in their relationship with Christ. He lives in Cincinnati with his two dogs Baxter and Buster. For more information on Billy's ministry, feel free to contact him through his website: *BillyHuddleston.com*.

www.ingramcontent.com/pod-product-compliance
Lightning Source LLC
LaVergne TN
LVHW010052110826
845155LV00028B/305

* 9 7 8 1 9 5 3 2 8 5 8 7 4 *